ALSO BY CHARLES A. WHITNEY

The Discovery of Our Galaxy (1971)

Whitney's Star Finder

WHITNEY'S

 Alfred A. Knopf • New York • 1989

STAR FINDER

A Field Guide to the Heavens

CHARLES A. WHITNEY

THIS IS A BORZOI BOOK
PUBLISHED BY ALFRED A. KNOPF, INC.

Published in the United States by Alfred A. Knopf,
Inc., New York, and simultaneously in Canada by
Random House of Canada Limited, Toronto.
Distributed by Random House, Inc., New York.
Grateful acknowledgment is made to Dover
Publications, Inc., for permission to reprint material
from Canon of Eclipses (Oppolzer); W. H. Freeman
and Company for a letter from Adm. G. L. Schuyler
(pages 148–50) in the "Amateur Scientist," March,
1956. Copyright © 1956 by Scientific American, Inc.
All Rights Reserved; and to the Lick Observatory,
University of California, Santa Cruz, for use of a
photograph of the Great Nebula of Orion.
Library of Congress Cataloging-in-Publication Data
Whitney, Charles Allen.
Whitney's Star finder.
Includes index.
1. Astronomy—Charts, diagrams, etc.
2. Astronomy—Observers' manuals. I. Title.
QB65.W48 1985   523   85–40349
ISBN 0–679–72582–2

Manufactured in the United States of America
First edition, June 1974
Second edition, October 1977
Third edition, October 1981
Fourth edition, October 1985
Fifth edition, October 1989

*Dedicated to the memory of
my brother,
who taught me how to skin a snake*

Contents

remaining until sunrise and sunset; Twilight colors; The shape and size of the setting sun; The midnight suns

Figures

Tables

Preface

This is a field guide to the sky. It does not attempt to explain astronomical knowledge or the ways in which astronomers study the sky. It attempts to explain the sky itself.

Friends often ask me, "What was that bright thing I saw last night?" I have written this book for them, and I hope it will help them find the answer right then, when they can take another look—and before they need to put me on the spot. I have limited myself to objects that are visible to most campers or might be of interest to those who merely wish to step outside for a few minutes with a small telescope or a pair of binoculars.

A special feature is the star finder in the back of this book. With this you will be able to predict the positions of the stars for any hour of any day, and you will be able to tell time by the stars and predict the time of sunset.

This book will also help you see the moon and Venus in broad daylight or catch a glimpse of the Andromeda galaxy and the Orion nebula. If you wish to know why Venus becomes bright in the evening sky and then jumps to the morning sky, turn to Chapter 3. That chapter will also help you see the moons of Jupiter with binoculars. The appendixes provide lists of coming events in the sky.

To cast your horoscope, locate the planets with the information in the Almanac of the Planets, and ask someone what it all means. This book will not help you interpret your horoscope. Sorry.

C. A. WHITNEY

Weston, Massachusetts
September 1973

Preface to the Fifth Edition

This is the first edition to contain the newly designed Pop-up sky, which represents the entire celestial sphere on a fourteen-sided polyhedron. It is found in the pocket inside the front cover.

The tables in this edition cover the interval 1990–95. I have added many new diagrams to help you identify the planets and find some interesting variable stars. Some of these diagrams were generated with an Apple Macintosh version of a computer program called Voyager, the Interactive Desktop Planetarium, which is available from Carina Software, 830 Williams Street, San Leandro, California 94577; telephone (415)352-7328.

Using This Book:
How Your Location Affects
the Appearance of the Sky

This book will help you find the stars and planets from any place in the world. You need only to know whether you are in the Northern or Southern Hemisphere and then choose the appropriate side of the star finder wheel. If you are in the Northern Hemisphere, it makes little difference whether you are in the United States, Europe, India, or Asia. And, if you are in the Southern Hemisphere, you can use the south side of the wheel in Africa, South America, Australia, or the islands of the South Pacific.

Moving eastward or westward at the same distance from the equator merely takes you into other time zones, and it hardly affects the appearance of the stars and planets. If you fly westward, chasing the sun, your day will be longer, and it will be shorter if you fly eastward. (I remember how short the night seemed when I flew eastward over the North Atlantic not long ago. The sun came up only a few hours after it had set, because we were racing to meet it.) The pole star stays at the same height in the sky, and the familiar constellations remain visible.

Suppose you started from Boston at noon and flew eastward at 750 miles per hour. This velocity would take you around the circle of latitude and return you to Boston in twenty-four hours, but you would have seen two sunrises during that time. Your day would seem half as long as an ordinary day for a person on the ground. On such a trip the North Star would stay at the same height in the sky, and the familiar constellations would be visible. In other words, eastward travel merely takes you into other time zones.

And if you traveled *westward* from Boston at 750 miles per hour, the sun would remain overhead the entire time. Over the Pacific Ocean you would cross the International Date Line and would have to tear a page off your calendar. In twenty-four hours you would have returned to Boston and a new day would have arrived, but you would have seen no sunset.

Suppose, on the other hand, you went to the North Pole. The North Star would be directly overhead, and the constellations would circle the horizon without rising or setting. The sun would rise and set once a year, and the moon once a month. Half of the sky would be perpetually invisible, and you would never see Orion, for example, because it lies below the equator.

Now imagine you head for the South Pole. The North Star gradually sinks toward the northern horizon—one degree for every 67 miles—and new constellations appear. As you cross the equator, the North Star vanishes and you notice that the stars are rotating about the South Pole of the sky, but clockwise rather than counterclockwise as they do in the north. Also, you will find winter when you had previously found summer, and spring in place of autumn.

The southern sky has neither a pole star nor a Big Dipper to mark it, but it makes up for these with a gallery of its own—the star clouds named after the explorer Magellan (who was the first European to describe them), the remarkable "globular" star cluster in Centaurus, and the glowing center of our own galaxy.

Although the star background changes as you travel south, several aspects of the sky remain unaltered. First, the sun would continue to cross your meridian at noon (or very nearly at noon) on your watch every day. You would remain in the same time zone. Also, the phases of the moon would be unaltered by your travel, and eclipses would occur on the same nights. The planets would remain among the same stars, and Venus, for example, would still be a morning or evening "star," as it had been in the other hemisphere. You might notice that the moon had moved a degree or two northward, but none of the planets would be sensibly shifted unless you observed them with a powerful telescope.

So, no matter where you intend to fish the skies, this book can help you get started.

USING THE POP-UP SKY

The pocket inside the front cover a contains a star chart printed on a fourteen-sided polyhedron that approximates the celestial sphere. The face of the pocket bears instructions on its use.

USING THE STAR FINDER

The pocket inside the rear cover contains a star finder wheel. The face of the pocket bears instructions on its use.

Whitney's Star Finder

What Is That Bright Object?

STREETS AND TRAFFIC IN THE SKY

Learning one's way among the stars is like learning one's way through the streets of an unfamiliar city. We start at a prominent intersection and move along boulevards and thoroughfares, progressing gradually to the lesser streets and alleys. We look for landmarks, but we ignore cars, trucks, and pedestrians, because many of them will have moved before we return to the same spot.

In much the same way, many constellations of stars are easily recognized: Orion, the Big Dipper, the **W** of Cassiopeia, the Southern Cross. These may serve as landmarks, but the moon and the planets are pedestrians, and we often find them in unexpected quarters. Comets are the foreigners, and they appear in strange clothing. Their behavior seems eccentric, and although they are inclined to avoid other pedestrians, they respond enthusiastically to the light of the sun. Meteors are their gypsy children, brilliant and unpredictable. They move in packs and rarely leave the orbits of their parents, nor do they often touch ground.

This chapter discusses the first step in reading the map of the sky: orienting yourself so you will not be caught holding the map upside down.

ORIENTATION

Because the North Star (Polaris) is nearly stationary in the sky, the ancient Egyptians thought it pointed the way to the realm of perpetual life. For the same reason, the North Star is the best reference point for orienting yourself on the sky when you are north of the equator. It is fairly bright, and it stands alone about halfway to the zenith from the northern horizon, forming the tip of the handle of the Little Dipper. If you find this constellation, you can be sure of your identification, but it is not a very bright group of stars, and I usually find the North Star in other ways.

The easiest way is to use the Big Dipper. If you find it, your problem is solved, because the end stars in the bowl of the Big Dipper always point directly to the North Star, as you can verify with the star finder in this book.

There are many other clues, and these may be useful if the Big Dipper is hidden. In particular, there are many constellations that have a well-defined "north side." The top of Orion, for example, always indicates the direction of the North Star. And if you find Cassiopeia and turn your head so it looks like a proper **W**, you will find the North Star toward the top of your head. Leo, the Lion, lies in the sky so that the North Star is above his back. You can discover a number of other indicators.

Even without using any of the constellations, you can find north if you lie on your back under a tree for a few minutes and watch a star near the zenith. (The tree branches make a good reference.) Within a few minutes, you will be able to detect the motion of this star caused by the rotation of the Earth. The star moves westward.

Orientation is quite simple on a sunny day. At noon, standard time, the sun is in the south, but if you would rather not wait until noon you can find south in a few minutes with a method borrowed from the *Scout Handbook*. This method uses the westward *motion* of the sun rather than the *position* of the sun at a particular time, and it will work well enough at any time of day, although it is most accurate around noon.

Find a pointed stick about four feet long. If you are in a rush, use one eight feet long—the shadow will move twice as fast. Jam it into the ground so that it points more or less upward and put a small stone at the tip of the stick's shadow. Now wait a few minutes. As the sun moves west, the shadow will move directly east, and when it has gone a few inches, put another stone at the tip of the shadow. The two stones lie east and west of each other. (That's not surprising. What *is* surprising is the speed of the shadow. If you did this using the shadow of the Eiffel Tower, the shadow would move seven feet per minute!)

FINDING SOUTH

Because the southern sky has no pole star as bright as Polaris, it is a bit tricky to determine directions quickly when you are south of the equator. You can, of course, lie on the ground to watch the westward motion of the stars, and then turn south.

But you can also use some of the more prominent constellations, and the best known of these is the Southern Cross, whose base points toward the South Pole.

USING THE STAR FINDER TO IDENTIFY STARS

This book contains a star finder which may be set for any hour of any day of the year. If you know the time and have found north, you are in a position to use the star finder to identify the stars. Set the date against the appropriate hour and hold the star finder over your head with the edge marked "south" pointing toward the south. In this position, it provides a map of the sky, and you will be able to pick out the constellations and the bright stars.

The stars return to the same positions each year. This is not true of the planets, and because they move among the stars, they are not shown on the finder. They must be handled in a different manner.

CAN IT BE A PLANET?

If a bright object is stationary and does not appear on the star finder, it may be a planet. With a telescope, you can easily identify the planets because each shows a disk, and the disks are all different. (The appearance of each planet is discussed in Chapter 3.) Without a telescope, it is often easier to tell what is *not* a planet than what *is.* Here are several ways you may be able to eliminate the planets from your list of suspects.

Does it twinkle? If the object shows strong twinkling, it probably is not a planet. Except for Mercury, the planets do not twinkle. (But neither do the stars when they are high overhead.)

Is it near the North Star or the South Pole? If so, it cannot be a planet. This is probably the one rule in this book that needs no qualification and has no exceptions. (Planetary orbits follow the path of the sun and never come within 50° of the North Star or the South Pole.)

If you are in the Northern Hemisphere and you see an object in the north, or high in the south, during the summer, it is probably not a planet. The orbits of the planets take them along the *ecliptic* (marked on the star finder), and this path puts them low in the south during the summer and high during the winter.

If you are in the Southern Hemisphere, the rule is reversed. There, the ecliptic path takes the planets low in the north during your summer and high during your winter. The simplest way to remember this is to recall that the planets are low in the sky at night during those seasons when the sun is high during the day.

COLORS AND BRIGHTNESSES OF THE PLANETS

Some planets have a distinctive color, and although the tints are not particularly striking, they are useful for identification. The colors are as follows:

PLANET	COLOR
Mercury	Silvery
Venus	Silvery
Mars	Reddish
Jupiter	White
Saturn	Yellowish

In addition to having a characteristic color, each planet also has a characteristic brightness. Although these brightnesses vary somewhat from season to season, they are helpful in identifying the planets. The following list compares each planet to Vega and Rigel, bright stars of the summer and winter sky, respectively.

PLANET	BRIGHTNESS RELATIVE TO VEGA AND RIGEL
Mercury	Similar
Venus	40×
Mars	4×
Jupiter	6×
Saturn	Similar

The planets cannot be placed on the star finder because they move swiftly among the stars, but here are some other clues you may use. Mercury will never be found outside twilight, and the times of its appearance are discussed in Chapter 3 and in the Almanac of the Planets. Venus is brighter than any other planet or star, so it is usually not difficult to identify with the clues in Chapter 3 and the Almanac of the Planets. To make a positive identification of Mars, Jupiter, or Saturn, you may turn to the Almanac of the Planets to find the planet's constellation at the moment and then locate that constellation on the star finder.

AIRPLANES AND ARTIFICIAL SATELLITES

Except for their motion, these objects often appear starlike. Binoculars will usually reveal the red and green wing lights of an airplane, but otherwise these objects are not easily distinguished. Both can show variations of brightness, and both can cross the sky in fifteen minutes or so. There are two ways to tell them apart. Airplanes can turn corners, while satellites rarely do. Also, satellites can vanish while high overhead, but airplanes rarely do. On a summer night, or near twilight in winter, you may see a satellite vanish into the shadow of the Earth. This is an eclipse, of sorts, and it is abrupt.

Finding the Moon

THE MONTH

Suppose the Earth stopped rotating and the sun became fixed in the sky on the western horizon just after sunset. The moon would then rise in the west once a month, move upward, and then set in the east. Because the full circle requires 29½ days, the moon would move about 12° eastward per day, slightly less than the spread of your fingers when you stretch your arm full length. At the time of the new moon, it passes within 5° of the sun—or less, depending on the orientation of the moon's orbit that month. About one day after new moon, the thin crescent appears in the evening twilight.

SEEING THE NEW MOON

We seldom notice the new moon until it is at least two days old, but with a little luck and a clear sky it can be seen a day earlier. Twenty-one hours after the time it passes nearest to the sun is the earliest you can expect to see it, and even then you will see it only for a short period after sunset. Binoculars will help.

SEEING THE MOON ANY DAY

Except near new moon, you can find the moon any day of the month by consulting the Phases of the Moon table in the back of this book.

When the new moon is "old" enough to be visible (two or three days), it will be found slightly east of the sun. It then sets shortly after sunset. One week after new moon, the moon is at "first quarter." Its face is half-illuminated and it is 90° east of the sun, so it rises in the east at noon and it sets at midnight. You will find it in the southeast portion of the sky during the afternoon.

On the night of full moon, you will see it opposite the sun; it rises at sunset and sets in the west at sunrise. Thus, you will not see the full moon in the daytime sky. Figure 1 shows the moon's phases in relation to its orbit and the direction of the sun.

Figure 1. A schematic representation of the moon's orbit around the Earth. Phases of the moon are labeled. Since the moon is spherical and orbits the Earth rather than the sun, it always appears as a crescent when it is near the sun.

One week after full moon, the moon is at third quarter, and it will be found 90° west of the sun. It then rises at midnight, is due south at sunrise, and sets at noon. You will find the third-quarter moon in the southwest portion of the sky during the morning.

With the table of lunar phases at the back of the book, you may estimate the phase of the moon on any day of the year. First quarter is one week after new moon, and third quarter is one week after full moon.

The phases of the moon do not repeat exactly from one *calendar* month to the next because the average length of the calendar month is one-twelfth of a year, or 30½ days, while the phases repeat every 29½ days. Thus, the full moon comes about one day earlier each month, on the average.

TABLE 1
CYCLE OF MOONRISES AND MOONSETS DURING A MONTH

PHASE	RISES AT:	SETS AT:
New moon	Sunrise	Sunset
First quarter	Noon	Midnight
Full moon	Sunset	Sunrise
Third quarter	Midnight	Noon

If you see a crescent moon in a painting or drawing, you can locate the sun and you can tell which direction the artist would have been facing, because the shape and tilt of the moon's face give clues to the time of month and the time of day. There are two types of clues. First, the side of the moon illuminated by the sun will always be sharp and round, because the moon is a tolerable sphere. This means the sun is in the direction indicated by the rounded side of the moon's face. Second, the sun's apparent distance across the sky is indicated by the width of the crescent or gibbous moon. For example, a thin crescent indicates that the sun is nearby. Figure 2 shows two examples.

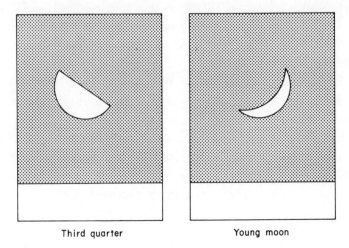

Third quarter   Young moon

Figure 2. The shape and tilt of the moon's crescent. From the shape and tilt of these crescents, you can determine the direction of view and the time. The third-quarter moon (left) has just risen, so the time is shortly after midnight and we are facing east. The young moon (right) is about to set, so the time is evening and we are facing west.

MOONRISE

The moon seldom follows precisely its "average" behavior. If it did, it would rise 50 minutes later each day, but the interval actually varies from 30 minutes to 75 minutes, and this variation makes it very difficult to guess the time of moonrise. Rather than give a complete table, I shall merely indicate some general rules, because newspapers often provide the times of moonrise and moonset with the weather forecast.

The moon moves north and south across the celestial equator during its monthly motion eastward around the Earth. The total swing north and south is 45°, and the moon seldom rises in the exact east. The *position* of the moon's rising will influence the *time* of its rising. When the moon is moving southward, its time of rising is delayed 75 minutes each day, and when it is moving northward, the delay is only 30 minutes. (This rule is reversed in the Southern Hemisphere.)

Whether you are in the Northern or the Southern Hemisphere, you will experience the "harvest moon" during your late summer and early autumn. In these seasons, the moon is moving rapidly across the equator, and its time of rising is delayed far less from one day to the next than at the other seasons. (Thirty minutes, instead of the typical value of fifty minutes or so.) The result is that the moon seems to linger in the sky, accommodating those who are outside at night. The moon nearest the fall equinox is the harvest moon. A month later, the "hunter's moon" behaves in a similar way.

HEIGHT OF THE FULL MOON

The full moon rises opposite the sun at sunset, so the behavior of the full moon is contrary to that of the sun. It is highest in winter and lowest in summer, shifting north and south in much the manner of the planets. (There is a slight additional difference arising from the tilt of the moon's orbit, but this is scarcely noticeable.) In December, when the sun is farthest south, the full moon is farthest north. (See Figure 3.)

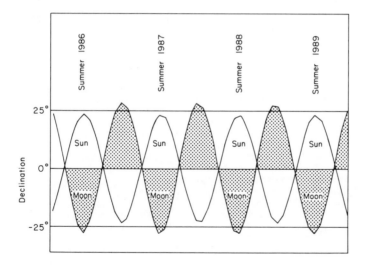

Figure 3. Variations in the height of the sun and the moon during the past decade. This diagram shows the declination of the moon at the time of full moon over a period of four years and indicates that the full moon is lower in summer, when the sun is high. This behavior is true in both hemispheres.

ASHEN LIGHT OF THE MOON

Near the time of new moon (either morning or evening), the full face of the moon can usually be seen within the thin crescent. This is called the "old moon in the new moon's arms," or the "ashen light." To understand it, imagine you are standing on the surface of the moon at this time. You will see a "full Earth," that is, the face of the Earth will be fully lit by the sun, and it will be more than ten times as bright as our full moon. The "moonscape" around you will be so brightly lit that it will be visible from the Earth as the "old moon in the new moon's arms." Careful observation of this ashen light shows that it varies from time to time. It is brightest on the evenings when the moon side of the Earth is most covered with clouds, which brightly reflect sunlight into space. ·

Observing the Planets with Binoculars

THE APPEARANCE AND MOTION OF THE PLANETS

The planets shine by light reflected from the sun, and one or more of them can be seen on most clear nights. Their apparent positions change very little from one part of the Earth to another, but over a period of a week it is possible to detect their motion if you locate them carefully among the stars.

The solar system is remarkably flat, and the planets remain within a narrow path, the "zodiac," because they lie within a single plane, like marbles resting on the top of a table—or nearly so. This plane also contains the Earth and the sun, and if we viewed it edge-on from one of the stars of the zodiac, we would see the planets strung out in a line. Only if we were to see the planets from a star far above or below the zodiacal circle would we see the roundness of their orbits about the sun.

As an example, Figures 4a and 4b show the planets as seen from Neptune, and they are strung out like beads on a string, except for Uranus, which is slightly wayward because of the tilt of its orbit.

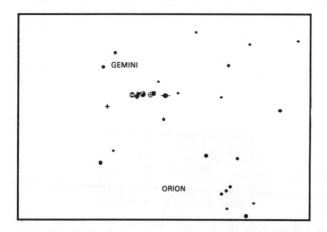

4a. The solar system seen from the planet Neptune on October 10, 1990. With the exception of Uranus (+), the planets appear along a line against the star-background of Gemini and Orion. This appearance results from the flatness of the solar system. See Figure 4b for a detailed view.

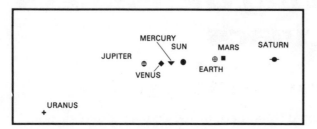

Figure 4b. The planets and the sun as seen from Neptune. These symbols will be used in other figures.

The flatness of the solar system and the roundness of the orbits suggest that the planets were formed from a nebula rotating about the sun. According to the most popular theory, solid particles within the nebula came together to form larger particles and sweep up the drifting gases. Only the largest survived. Around each of them a similar swarm of particles formed the satellites. If current thinking is correct, the formation of planets around stars may be a fairly common occurrence, and recent infrared observations from a space telescope have shown flattened clouds of particles around several of the nearer stars. These are probably solar systems in the process of condensation.

The Earth is the third of the known planets: Mercury, Venus, Earth, Mars, Jupiter, Saturn, Uranus, Neptune, Pluto. The first six were known to ancients, and the remaining three were discovered in modern times by a combination of computation, acuity, and luck. William Herschel discovered Uranus in 1781 while scanning the sky with a telescope. He thought he had discovered a comet until its subsequent motion proved otherwise. The existence of Neptune was postulated to explain the peculiar irregularities in the motion of Uranus, and it was discovered in 1846. In a similar fashion, irregularities in the motion of Neptune stimulated a search for a ninth planet, and the search ended with Clyde Tombaugh's discovery of Pluto in 1930. (Oddly enough, the predictions on which Tombaugh based his search were later shown to have been incorrectly computed, although they gave the correct result.)

Peculiarities in the motion of Halley's Comet were recently interpreted as indicating the presence of a tenth planet, beyond Pluto, but further analysis showed that the hypothetical planet would have disturbed the other planets out of their present orbits. The conclusion is that Halley's Comet is disturbed by the impulse of gas being ejected from its body.

The last three planets are more difficult. Pluto requires at least a twenty-four-inch telescope and special star charts. Ways to find Uranus and Neptune are discussed later in this chapter.

Planets nearer than the Earth to the sun behave quite differently from the outer planets. The inner planets remain fairly close to the sun because we see their orbits from the outside. The maximum angles are 28° for Mercury and 46° for Venus. The outer planets, on the other hand, may be found at any angle from the sun.

Another feature distinguishing the behavior of these two groups is that the inner planets can show crescents like the moon's, while the outer planets always appear nearly full.

All planets move about their orbits in the same direction: counterclockwise when seen from the North Star. This is also the direction of the Earth's daily rotation and the rotation of the other visible planets with the exception of Venus.

The outer planets move much more slowly than the inner planets. (Their years are longer, and they move fewer miles per hour.) There is a regular progression, explained by Isaac Newton in terms of the sun's gravitational field, so if the planets were one day lined up like spots on the spoke of a wheel, the inner ones would quickly move ahead. Thus, the planets are continually rearranging themselves.

The Almanac of the Planets at the end of this book gives some details that, along with the charts in this chapter, will help you keep track of the planets.

ORBITS OF THE INNER PLANETS: MERCURY AND VENUS

If we were far above the solar system looking down on the North Pole of the Earth, the orbit of Venus would resemble the circle in Figure 5. The orbital motion of Venus and the Earth, as well as the daily rotation of the Earth, are counterclockwise in this figure, so Venus will be seen in the evening sky when it is on the left-hand side of the sun. (Think about that for a minute. Eastward is counterclockwise in this view, so evening objects are to the left of the sun.) When Venus overtakes the Earth and passes nearly in front of the sun (inferior conjunction), it vanishes for about three weeks in the twilight and reappears in the morning sky—to the west of the sun. Thus, the moment of its passage from evening to morning sky is also the moment of its closest approach to the Earth. And it is the time of its thinnest crescent.

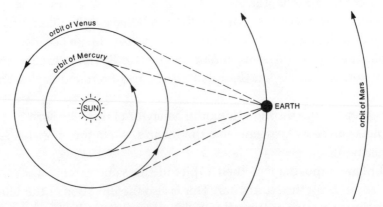

Figure 5. The orbits of Mercury, Venus, Earth, and Mars, as seen from above the solar system. Because Mercury and Venus are closer to the sun than the Earth is, they remain near the sun in the sky. Mars, in an outer orbit, occasionally lies opposite the sun—approximately every two years.

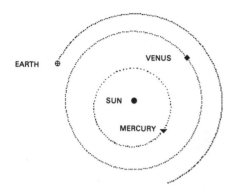

EARTH ⊕

SUN ●

VENUS ◆

MERCURY ▾

Figure 6. In this view looking down on the solar system, we see that planets closer to the sun move more rapidly. During one of Venus's years, Earth moves only 0.6 of an orbit while Mercury moves 2.6 orbits.

SEEING MERCURY

Relatively few people notice Mercury. Its orbit size is only two-fifths that of the Earth's orbit, and Mercury is never more than 28° or about two hand-widths from the sun. It must be hunted in the twilight.

Look for Mercury within a week of its greatest eastward (evening) or westward (morning) elongations from the sun. It is then seen as a zero-magnitude star, similar to Vega, and it can be spotted quite easily with a pair of binoculars. You will not see its disk without a magnification of at least $50\times$.

Figure 7 is a schematic representation of the appearance of Mercury as seen from above the Earth's orbit. The planet Mercury is more easily seen at some elongations than at others.

Mercury has a very thin atmosphere that it may have captured from gases flowing out from the sun, and the daytime temperature of its surface is high enough to melt lead. The markings of its surface are very difficult to see from the Earth, but the Mariner 10 fly-by revealed numerous craters similar to the moon's.

The rotation period of Mercury is not, as had been thought, equal to its orbital period of eighty-eight days. Radar observations show that it is two-thirds of that, or fifty-nine days. Thus, the planet rotates one and a half times in a single year, and three rotations require two years! This, and the fact that Mercury's orbit is the most eccentric of any planet, would lead to a peculiar daytime experience for sojourners on the planet, as has been pointed out by Lawrence E. Turner, Jr. (*American Journal of Physics*, **46**, 475, 1978). During most of Mercury's orbit, the

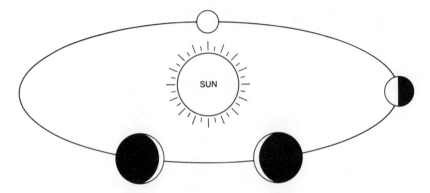

Figure 7. A schematic view from above the Earth's orbit, showing the appearance of Mercury as it moves about the sun. The portion illuminated by the sun is crescent-shaped when Mercury is near the Earth; it becomes a half-circle when Mercury is at greatest elongation from the sun; and it is gibbous when Mercury is on the far side of its orbit. Note the changes of size accompanying the changes of distance from Earth. These changes of Mercury's appearance require a moderate telescope. Similar phenomena occur for Venus and are not difficult to see with a securely mounted pair of 7X binoculars or a small telescope. They formed one part of Galileo's argument in the seventeenth century for the sun-centered solar system.

sun will behave conventionally, rising in the east, moving slowly across the sky, and setting in the west. But when the planet is closest to the sun, its orbital motion speeds up. The result is that the sun will appear to move backward on the sky for about eight Earth days, looping from west to east before moving westward again toward the sunset. An extraordinary opportunity for sunbathing!

VENUS, THE EVENING AND MORNING STAR

Venus comes nearest to the Earth, and it has the brightest face of any planet. Its brilliant silver light is unmistakable in the twilight, and it may also be seen during the day throughout much of the year.

At intervals of nineteen months Venus reaches maximum height in the evening sky when it is at its greatest eastward distance from the sun, and its face has the appearance of the moon at first quarter. A month later it begins to fade and finally vanishes in the glare of the sun, where it is lost for about three weeks.

Then it reappears in the morning sky and rises higher each day before being lost in the glare of the rising sun. Two months later, it is at its greatest westward distance from the sun and it stands high in the morning sky at dawn. Then it again vanishes into the glare of sunrise and remains invisible for two months, reappearing in the evening sky and repeating the cycle. By a remarkable coincidence, thirteen Venus years equal eight Earth years (less one day), so this seasonal cycle of Venus repeats every eight years.

Venus Orbitting the Sun   Venus in P.M. Sky

Figure 8. The crescents of Venus in the twilight. A schematic representation of Venus in orbit (left) and in the twilight sky (right), showing how its distance from the sun will be related to the shape of its crescent. Similar phenomena occur for Mercury, although they are much more difficult to see.

The diagrams in Figure 9 will help you keep track of Venus. These are views of the solar system as seen from above: by drawing lines from the Earth to the sun and to a planet, you can determine the directions to these objects as seen from Earth. A useful rule to remember is that when a planet as seen from the Earth is to the right of the sun, it is in the morning sky; when it is to the left of the sun, it is in the evening sky. (It may be helpful to think of the phrase "right on until morning.")

Venus shows a changing crescent that can be seen quite well with a telescope magnification of 7× or 10×. Binoculars will work if they are securely mounted. This crescent has the same origin as that of our moon, but the two crescents will generally have different shapes, even when they are seen in the same part of the sky. For example, if you see Venus in the evening sky near the thin crescent of the new moon, Venus may have either a full face or a thin crescent.

The silvery luster of Venus is produced by a thick, hot atmosphere of carbon dioxide nearly one hundred times as dense as the atmosphere of the Earth. Winds of 200 miles per hour blow continually around the planet, so rapidly that there is no difference between daytime and nighttime temperature near the surface. Radar signals have revealed extensive mountain ranges beneath the clouds.

Figure 9. Views looking down on the solar system on the indicated dates. The relative positions of the planets are shown to scale, so these diagrams may be used to estimate the angular positions of the planets as seen from any point. By drawing lines from the Earth to the sun and a planet, the angle between those objects may be measured. When a planet is nearly aligned with the sun, it will be lost in daylight. The track in each diagram corresponds to ¼ year, or 3 months.

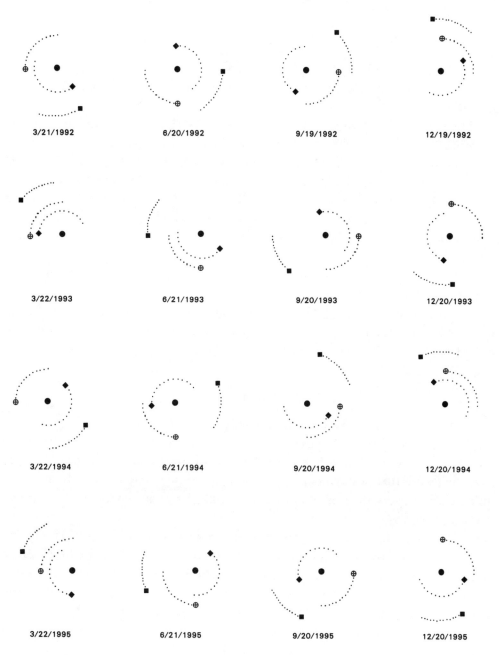

3/21/1992   6/20/1992   9/19/1992   12/19/1992

3/22/1993   6/21/1993   9/20/1993   12/20/1993

3/22/1994   6/21/1994   9/20/1994   12/20/1994

3/22/1995   6/21/1995   9/20/1995   12/20/1995

SEEING VENUS AND SIRIUS IN THE DAYTIME

Unlike any other planet, Venus may be seen by the naked eye in full daylight for several months around the times of its greatest apparent distance from the sun.

For my first attempt at seeing Venus in the daylight, I watched it in the morning twilight just before dawn and measured its distance from the sun using my extended fingers. (This distance remains constant as the two objects move across the sky during the day.) Later in the morning, I swept the suspected location of Venus with a pair of binoculars, and when I found it I pinpointed its location against the branches of a tree. Then I lowered my binoculars and, in a moment, the planet jumped out at me. I wondered why I had not seen it sooner.

Sirius, the brightest star in the sky, is about one-tenth the typical brightness of Venus, and it may also be seen in full daylight, but you'll need a telescope. If you point a three-inch, or greater, telescope accurately at the location of Sirius, you will see it without much difficulty. I have tried to find Sirius with a 1½-inch pair of binoculars, but without success.

MARS

Mars's unblinking reddish light makes it fairly easy to find among the stars. The orbit of Mars lies outside the Earth's and it can be seen directly opposite the sun every two years, when it is closest to the Earth. Even then, its disk is only one-hundredth that of the moon, so a good pair of binoculars will barely show the disk. A telescope with a magnification of 200× is required to see its surface markings.

Mars's motion on the sky is quite different from that of Venus and Mercury. At opposition it rises at sunset and can be seen all night. Two months before opposition it rises at midnight and can be seen in the southeastern part of the sky for several hours before dawn. Two months after opposition it is seen in the evening sky and it sets at midnight. (Jupiter and Saturn do much the same, but their oppositions occur nearly every year.)

The motion of Mars among the bright stars can be seen by the naked eye if you watch for a week or so. This motion appears rather erratic.

The diagrams in Figure 9 will permit you to determine the position of Mars (as well as Venus) relative to the sun at any time in the interval 1990–95.

For most of the year, Mars moves eastward among the stars at a rate of about 20° per month, but when it approaches opposition it slides backward about 15° in two months. This is its "retrograde motion," and it is caused by the orbital motion of the Earth. It is a consequence of our perspective. If the Earth were stationary (an impossibility in the neighborhood of the sun), Mars would move continually eastward and circle the sky in twenty-three months. Because the Earth moves fairly rapidly, Mars is overtaken every twenty-six months, and it falls behind for a while.

MODERN VERSION OF THE "CANALS" OF MARS

Photographs of Mars from space satellites and landers have revealed enormous volcanic craters, and many long valleys resembling dried riverbeds. Water erosion was very extensive at some time in the past, and all of the water now appears to be trapped in the polar caps, and perhaps under the ground. None of these features explains the "canals" reported at the beginning of this century. They were evidently the result of optical illusions. The surface of Mars is reddish and strewn with broken rocks. Even the sky appears pink from the ground.

Mars is 100°F cooler than the Earth because it is farther from the sun, and this difference will someday make Mars an attractive place to live, because the sun is growing brighter and will warm the Earth beyond the comfort point in a few billion years—according to current theories.

JUPITER

Jupiter excels all other planets in size, number of moons, speed of daily rotation, markings, and availability to the observer with binoculars or a small telescope. Jupiter is second to Venus in brightness. Its orbit about the sun is five times larger than the Earth's and requires twelve years, so the planet moves along at an average rate of one zodiacal constellation per year. Thus, Jupiter will be seen at opposition about one month later each year. Like Saturn it may be seen in the evening sky five months of the year and in the morning sky five months. The remaining two months are lost to the light of the sun. (See Figure 10.)

Figure 10. Planets farther from the sun move more slowly. During one Earth year, Mars moves 1/2 of an orbit while Jupiter moves 1/12 and Saturn moves 1/30. As seen from Earth, Jupiter moves one zodiacal constellation per year and Saturn moves about half as fast around the sky.

Four of Jupiter's moons would be visible with the naked eye if it were not for the glare of Jupiter's light, and they can often be seen with a good pair of binoculars mounted on a very steady support. The moons appear to lie on a straight line and to move back and forth along this line. Thus, the number of moons on each side of Jupiter will vary from night to night. The two inner moons move rapidly, and their motions can be seen during a single night, but the outer two move very little from one night to the next. The period of each moon is determined by the mass of Jupiter and by the moon's distance from Jupiter. (The moon's mass is irrelevant as long as it is small.) A similar relationship holds for the planets; their orbital periods depend only on the mass of the sun and the planet's distance from the sun. These relationships are explained by Newton's law of gravity.

The Voyager spacecraft detected a thin ring around Jupiter, invisible from Earth, and astronomers have also detected a faint narrow ring around Uranus, so Saturn is no longer unique in this way.

Jupiter rotates so rapidly (once in ten hours) that a patient observer with a five-inch or ten-inch telescope can see the movement of its clouds in a few hours. It has an intense magnetic field and its upper atmosphere discharges enormous lightning bolts. One of the most fascinating discoveries by the spacecraft is that Jupiter's satellite, Io, sprays gas into space from active volcanoes. These are the only known volcanoes outside the Earth. Like Saturn, Jupiter emits more energy than it receives from the sun, probably as a result of a slow shrinking that heats the interior. The cause of Jupiter's Great Red Spot is still unknown, but the gases can be seen swirling rapidly inside it.

Figure 11. The track of Jupiter along the zodiac, 1990–93. By using this diagram (or the next) to locate Jupiter among the stars on the star finder wheel, it is possible to determine when the planet will be visible. Note that Jupiter moves through one constellation per year. The positions shown correspond to February 1 each year.

SATURN

Saturn moves more slowly than Jupiter, and it circles the zodiac in thirty years, so you will see it in the same constellation for more than a year at a time. Also, its orbit is nearly circular and ten times larger than the Earth's, so its distance

Figure 12. The track of Jupiter along the zodiac, 1993–97. (See caption to Figure 11.)

from us changes relatively little. Saturn shows no crescent (nor do Mars and Jupiter, for that matter), and it always appears nearly the same size in a telescope.

The moons of Saturn are invisible with binoculars, and its surface is hidden beneath a layer of clouds. Galileo's telescope was not much better than present-day binoculars, and when he first examined Saturn he thought it had "ears" or lobes on each side. Part of Galileo's difficulty was that he did not *expect* to see rings. You will probably have a somewhat easier time of it, but magnification of 25× or more is required to see the rings clearly.

The Voyager explorations of Saturn revealed that the rings are far more complicated than astronomers had guessed. Each of the major rings is divided into hundreds of finer rings, and the inner ones rotate more rapidly. Beyond the bright rings is a faint ring that is surely one of the most remarkable features of the solar system. It looks like a braid of strings, twisted around each other and looped around the planet. No convincing explanations have been offered as of this writing. Another remarkable discovery is that one of the larger divisions appears to have at least one small satellite in it, in addition to some previously unseen matter, and one popular theory is that the moon acts to "herd" the particles and hold them in the region of the division, which was previously thought to be empty. Saturn also has bands in its atmosphere and a faint reddish spot similar to Jupiter's.

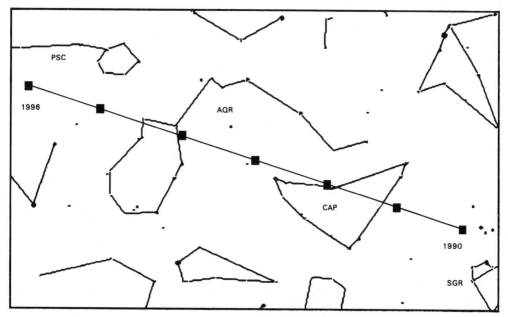

Figure 13. The track of Saturn along the zodiac, 1990–96. By using this diagram to locate Saturn among the stars on the star finder wheel, it is possible to determine when the planet will be visible. Saturn moves through one constellation in about 2.5 years. The positions shown correspond to mid-August each year.

URANUS AND NEPTUNE

Uranus is near the limit of naked-eye visibility, but you should be able to find it easily with binoculars and the chart in Figure 14. Neptune is typically 8th magnitude, making it a somewhat more difficult object. Its position is also shown in Figure 14. Its angular size from the Earth is similar to that of Uranus (30 arc-seconds, or about 1/60 the angular size of the moon), so it can be identified with a telescope whose magnification (50×) is sufficient to show the disc and

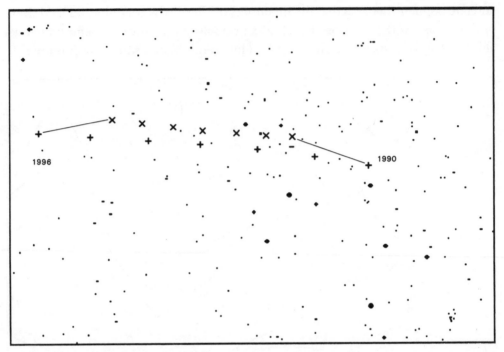

Figure 14. The tracks of Uranus and Neptune along the zodiac, 1990–96. Uranus is about magnitude 5 and it can be seen easily with binoculars. Neptune can be seen under fine conditions. (See text for hints on finding Neptune.) Note the greater speed of Uranus, which is closer to the Earth and the sun. Stars are plotted to about magnitude 8, which is the brightness of Neptune.

distinguish it from stars, which do not show discs. Without a telescope, you may be able to find Neptune with binoculars by carefully mapping all the stars in the neighborhood of the expected location indicated in Figure 14. After a month, you should be able to detect its motion.

PLANETARY ALIGNMENT OF 1991

In the early summer of 1991, the six planets Mercury, Venus, Earth, Mars, Jupiter, and Saturn will be arranged in a very unusual alignment, as shown in

Figures 15–17. As seen from Earth, Mercury, Venus, Mars, and Jupiter will appear in the evening sky and will all be visible to the naked eye. The new moon will be seen with these planets in the twilight of July 12, 1991. Saturn is on the opposite side of the Earth from the other planets, so it will rise at approximately sunset.

This alignment should be viewed merely as a curiosity of significance only for astrology. Such alignments are bound to occur from time to time, and they have no physical or astronomical significance. Aside from providing a splendid display in the sky, they do not affect the Earth in any measurable fashion. A similar alignment (although not quite as tightly arranged) took place in 1931. And in October 1946, the planets Mercury, Venus, Mars, and Jupiter were visible together in the evening twilight.

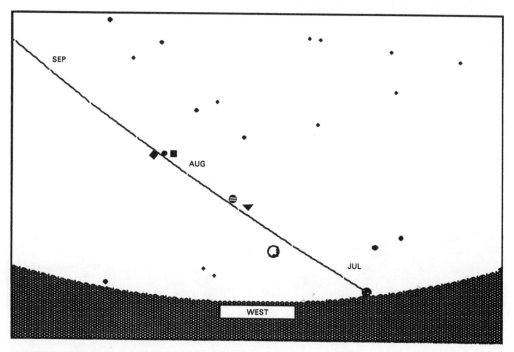

Figure 15. The evening sky: view looking west on July 12, 1991. For several weeks around this time, the planets are closely aligned (see Figure 16) and will appear as an elongated cluster in the sky.

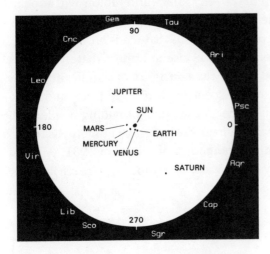

Figure 16. View looking down on the solar system at the time of the unusual alignment of July 1991. All the visible planets are arranged along a single line for a space of a few weeks.

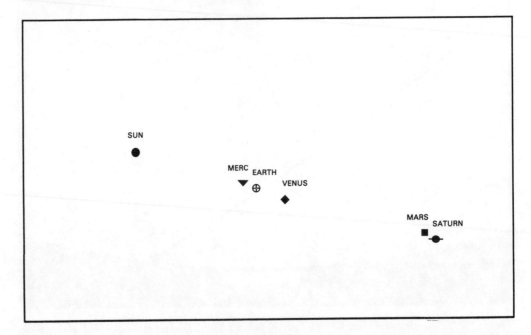

Figure 17. View of the solar system as seen from Jupiter during the alignment of early July 1991.

4

Determining Time by the Sun and Stars

NATURAL CLOCKS

The sky provides a number of clocks, and the most obvious is the sun. Our *civil* clocks (the kind we find in grocery stores) are set to sun time, and their hour hands rotate twice while the sun rotates once around the sky. The rotation of the moon about the Earth defines the month, and the rotation of the Earth about the sun defines the year. (Longer cycles can also be discerned. For example, the rotation of the sun about the center of the Milky Way defines the "cosmic year" of about 200,000 terrestrial years.)

This chapter will consider three types of time determination: the hour during the day, the hour during the night, and the season of the year. They depend only on the motion of the sun and stars, and there will be no further mention of the planets or the moon in this chapter.

SUN TIME AND TIME ZONES

Civil clocks mark twenty-four hours while the sun makes a complete revolution of the sky (360°), so the sun moves 15° per hour. (See Figure 18.) For an observer at the center of his time zone, the sun is directly south at noon; it is 90° eastward at 6 a.m.; it is 90° westward in its cycle of the sky at 6 p.m. (This assumes standard time. During daylight-saving time these events occur one hour later.)*

6 a.m.   Noon   6 p.m.

Figure 18. Solar time. The sun, indicated by the circle, moves westward across the sky in about 12 hours, and it is due south at noon. Thus the eastward or westward distance from due south indicates the time before or after noon.

For an observer who is not at the center of his time zone, the situation is slightly different. If he is *east* of the center, the events occur at an *earlier* civil time. For example, Cleveland and Boston are in the Eastern Time Zone, but the sun rises forty minutes earlier in Boston, because Boston is 10° of longitude eastward, toward the rising sun.

The time zones are spaced at 15° intervals around the globe, and the sun moves from one to the next in an hour. Boston is 71° west of Greenwich, England (where it all begins), so it is in the fifth zone. But it is 4° east of the center of its zone (75°), so its sun time is four-fifteenths of an hour, or sixteen minutes, ahead of Eastern Standard Time. Therefore the sun comes due south sixteen minutes

---

*There is a simple way to recollect the difference between standard and daylight-saving time: The clock *springs* forward to daylight-saving time in the spring, and it *falls* back to standard time in the fall.

earlier than our civil clocks would indicate. Knowing your own longitude, you can estimate the correction from civil time to sun time at your location, remembering *eastward* means the sun is early.

MAKING A SUNDIAL

The mathematical design of an accurate sundial is a fascinating and complex problem, but the practical procedure is very simple. It requires nothing but time, and the accuracy you achieve is mostly a matter of size. If you make yours large enough, you can time the boiling of eggs.

For the moment, I will assume you have a watch, because it simplifies the procedure, but I will later mention how it could be done with a compass. (Actually, you don't even need a compass, but again it simplifies matters if you have one.)

Find a thin stick about six feet long. Jam it into a piece of flat ground where the sun will shine most of the day, and collect a bunch of small sticks. Carve an hour number on each, and when your watch indicates that an hour has arrived, put the appropriate stick at the tip of the shadow of the large stick. Do something else for an hour, then put in another stick, and do this all day—or do it every half-hour or quarter-hour if you want more accuracy. If your stick is six feet long, the shadow will move about two feet east every hour, and more rapidly near sunset and sunrise.

This sundial will work all year, but as the seasons pass, and the sun's height increases and decreases, the shadow will fall at varying distances from the foot of the stick. You can put more hour sticks in after a week or so, and if you mark them with the date you will have a calendar as well as a clock.

A SUN CALENDAR-CLOCK IN YOUR HOUSE

An indoor sundial was described in the March 1956 issue of *Scientific American* by the late Rear Admiral Garret L. Schuyler, U.S.N. It takes advantage of a long sunbeam and is therefore more precise than most sundials, and it can be constructed on the ceiling of a bedroom—a clear advantage on a wintry morning.

Admiral Schuyler wrote, "First select a window sill which gets direct sunshine for a couple of hours each day. Inside the window, and well back on the horizontal sill-surface so as to avoid the shadow of the bottom of the window frame when the sun is low in the winter, stick a ⅝-inch-square mirror face upward, using Duco cement. The sun's rays will be reflected upward from this small mirror and, even if they should have to pass through a light rayon curtain, they will make a small, roundish spot of light which travels across the ceiling as the sun's position shifts.

"At some selected time of day, say noon, mark the position of the image on the ceiling with a tack or an inconspicuous cross. Record the date with this mark. Repeat the process at weekly intervals as the seasons change and the sun travels north or south. Now, if you draw a smooth curve on the ceiling through all the marked points, you will be able to tell noon of each day as the moment when the sun's image touches a point on this line. If you also mark its position on the curve on the first day of each month, you can closely estimate the day of the month from the image's crossing on any day.

"Such a curve, labeled 'analemma' and marked with the months of the year, is often reproduced on geographical globes in the conveniently open area of the Pacific Ocean. Our curve on the ceiling is this same analemma—reversed by reflection, distorted by oblique projection on the ceiling, and modified by two sudden displacements when the time changes from 'Standard Time' to 'Daylight Time' and vice versa. But even though the mirror is canted and the ceiling may be somewhat irregular, the method described will establish a time-of-day curve without resort to mathematics or the usual correction devices, required by sundials.

"A single line is perhaps all that many persons will want, but by constructing a series of lines corresponding to the hours and quarter-hour intervals one can readily make a complete sundial. Care must be taken, however, to distinguish the parts of the lines which are traced when the sun is traveling south (June to December) from those when it is traveling north (December to June). One set of markings may be traced by solid lines and the other by dotted lines. . . .

"The traveling spot corresponds to the sun's image in a pinhole camera, the 'pinhole orifice' being replaced by the small mirror. . . . If you watch carefully, cloud formations can often be seen drifting across the sun's disk. Thus the indoor sundial acts as a vane showing the direction of the wind. This effect could doubtless be heightened by inserting a [very weak] spectacle lens of appropriate focal length in the beam—but I have not added this refinement."

SETTING YOUR WATCH BY THE SUN

If your watch stops, you can use it as a sundial if it is the type with hands. This trick depends on the fact that the sun goes around once a day while the hour hand goes around twice as fast, completing two circles in a day.

Northern Hemisphere: First find south and hold the watch so the twelve o'clock mark points in that direction. Hold a matchstick vertically on the face of the watch and move it around the numbers on the dial until its shadow falls on the central pivot of the hands. (See Figure 19.) The true time interval until noon or since noon will be just twice the interval indicated by the position of the matchstick on the dial. For example, if the stick is at eleven o'clock (one hour from noon), the time is ten o'clock (two hours from noon).

Southern Hemisphere: Find north, and point the twelve o'clock mark in that direction. Again, hold a matchstick so the shadow falls on the pivot, and determine how many hours the shadow is from the twelve o'clock mark. Double that to find the number of hours from noon.

Figure 19. How to set a watch by the sun. With a compass, determine south and point the twelve o'clock in that direction. Hold a small stick upright and move it around the dial until its shadow falls on the central pivot. The time interval from noon, as indicated by considering the stick to be an hour hand, is just half the true interval from noon. In this figure, the true time is two hours before noon, or ten o'clock. (This method is based on the fact that the clock is so constructed that the hour hand moves a full circle in half a day; that is, it moves twice as fast as the sun.)

FINDING SOUTH AND NORTH
WITH YOUR WATCH AND THE SUN

If your watch is telling the correct time, you may use it to determine south by a modification of the method described in the preceding section. (Both methods depend on the fact that the hour hand moves 30° per hour while the sun moves 15° per hour.)

Hold a matchstick vertically on the face of the watch at a point just above the tip of the hour hand. Now rotate the watch until the shadow of the match falls on the central pivot of the hands. South will lie halfway between the hour hand and the twelve o'clock mark.

As an example, suppose it is six o'clock in the morning; the sun is due east, and according to the method described the twelve o'clock mark will be due west. South is halfway between.

Doing this in the Southern Hemisphere to find north is a little trickier, and trying to do it will make you realize that our clockwise watches are the result of standing in the north and watching the sun move left to right during the day. In the south it moves right to left if you face it in the northern part of the sky, so you have to pretend that your watch hands rotate in the counterclockwise direction. Hold the watch with the twelve o'clock mark pointing north and hold a stick, not over the actual hour hand, but the place it would be if the hands went counterclockwise. (That is, at two in the afternoon, hold the stick where the hand was two hours before noon—at ten o'clock.) Then rotate the watch until the shadow of the stick falls on the central pivot, and you will find north halfway between the matchstick and the twelve o'clock mark.

CONSTELLATIONS
AND SIGNS OF THE ZODIAC

Ancient astronomers divided the sun's path about the sky into twelve nearly equal portions and assigned a constellation to each. These are the constellations of the zodiac. ("Zodiac" means "circle of the animals," although not all of the constellations currently represent animals.) On a specific date each year, the sun returns to the same constellation and hides it from our view, so it is easier to determine where the sun is *not* than where it *is*. The following table lists the constellations of the zodiac that are on the meridian at midnight each month. (These constellations are opposite the sun on these dates, and six months later the sun will be *in* these constellations.)

MONTH	CONSTELLATION ON THE MERIDIAN AT MIDNIGHT ON THE 21ST OF EACH MONTH
January	Cancer
February	Leo
March	Virgo
April	Libra
May	Scorpius
June	Sagittarius
July	Capricornus
August	Aquarius
September	Pisces
October	Aries
November	Taurus
December	Gemini

The star finder shows the sun's path ("ecliptic") among the stars and indicates the precise locations of the sun on successive dates. You will find, for example, that the sun is in Capricornus in January—just six months after Capricornus was directly south at midnight. But if you know something about the astrological "signs" of the zodiac, you will see there is a discrepancy between the constellations and the signs. My birthday, for example, is in January, and I am said to be an "Aquarian" despite the fact that the sun is in Capricornus that month. Astrologers are aware of this discrepancy, and it doesn't seem to disturb them.

The shift between the signs and the constellations is caused by the "precession of the equinoxes," or the shift of the Earth's pole of rotation. Three thousand years ago—and perhaps longer—astronomers chose the sun signs according to the corresponding zodiacal constellations (or perhaps vice versa), and they set Aries at the spring equinox. But the Earth's axis of rotation has shifted since then, and the position of the sun on the first day of spring now lies in Pisces. One entire rotation about the zodiac requires 26,000 years, and in this time the north and south celestial poles will each inscribe a complete circle on the sky. Vega, in the constellation Lyra, was a fairly close pole star 14,000 years ago, and it will be again in another 12,000 years. The Southern Hemisphere has no star to mark its pole at the moment, although the base of the Southern Cross indicates its general direction. With time, the South Pole will swing toward the Milky Way and it will come quite close to the bright star Gamma Velorum in another 8,000 years. (Gamma is an extraordinarily hot star, and it is spraying its atmosphere into space, for reasons that are still a mystery.)

THE STAR CLOCK

The dial of the star clock is the zodiac, and the hour hand is your meridian, or north-south line. When the vernal equinox (Pisces) is on the meridian, the star time is zero hours, and each 15° eastward indicates another hour. Taurus, for example, is 60° east of Pisces, and it indicates four hours star time.

The star clock and the sun clock shift against each other as the sun moves eastward among the stars. If you observe the stars at the same sun time, say 9 p.m., you will notice the stars shift slightly westward each night, toward the setting sun. In the course of a year, the stars make one more rotation than the sun, so the star clock rotates more rapidly, by about 1° per day, and the stars set 3 minutes 56 seconds earlier each night than they did the night before. This difference accumulates to one day in a year.

The star clock and the sun clock agree on September 21. At midnight, for example, both clocks read zero hours of the new day. To compute the difference between these clocks at a later date, add 3 minutes 56 seconds for each day that has elapsed, remembering that the star time is *ahead* of sun time.

A precise knowledge of star time is required by those who wish to compute the direction to point their telescope for a particular star, but you will not ordinarily need it. Instead, you may estimate sun time directly from the star clock using the star finder in this book. The method is simple and is described in the next section.

FINDING THE SUN TIME FROM THE STARS
AND THE STAR FINDER

Knowing the date, you may find the sun time from the stars as follows. In the Northern Hemisphere, face south and hold the star finder up in front of you with the south portion of its horizon downward. In the Southern Hemisphere, face north and hold the star finder up in front of you with the north portion of its horizon downward. (From here on, it makes no difference which hemisphere you are in.) Rotate the star disk until it reproduces the observed positions of the stars. A particularly accurate method is to notice the heights of stars that are setting in the west and rising in the east. Then adjust the star finder until these relative heights are correctly reproduced. Now locate the date on the outer scale of the star finder and read the corresponding sun time on the adjacent scale. That's all there is to it.

As an example, Figure 20 shows the Big Dipper as it would appear during early September for an observer facing north. The orientation of the bowl indicates the time of night.

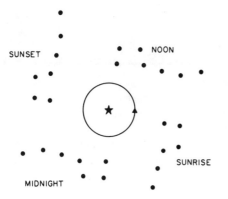

THE BIG DIPPER AS A CLOCK IN SEPTEMBER EVERY YEAR

Figure 20. Orientation of the Big Dipper during early September each year. This diagram shows how the orientation of the bowl is related to the time of night. Like the hand of a clock, the Dipper rotates once per day, and its position indicates the time. Similarly, the position at a particular time of night is an indication of the month. In this way, the stars have been used as a calendar. Other samples of this sort may be illustrated with the star finder furnished with this book.

The star finder can also be used to determine the date by observing the stars visible in the east just before sunrise. This is called the heliacal rising. (See Figure 21.) Set the star finder wheel so the eastern horizon is just beneath the rising stars and then read the date as the sun's path crosses the horizon.

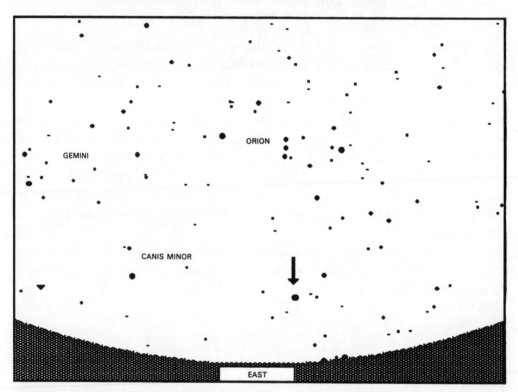

Figure 21. The heliacal rising of Sirius (arrow) in the dawn sky. Sirius is seen about 10° above the southeastern horizon just before the sun blots out the stars on August 13, 1992, from the location of Babylon (latitude 32° 33' N, longitude 44° 24' E). This pattern is characteristic of mid-August during the present century. In 1000 B.C. such a heliacal rising of Sirius would have occurred on the first of August, marking the start of the "dog days" of summer. The shift is caused by the precession of the equinoxes. The heliacal risings of other stars can be used to keep track of the seasons.

DETERMINING THE DATE
BY OBSERVING THE STARS AT TWILIGHT

Even if you do not have a watch and do not know the date, the position of the sun among the stars will tell you the date. Once the date is known, you can use the method of the preceding section to find the time, so the star finder can serve as a calendar as well as a watch.

The trick in determining the date is to find the sun's position among the stars, and twilight is a good time to do this because you can see the stars and you know the sun is just below the horizon.

At the start of morning twilight (about an hour before sunrise) note the positions of the stars, and set the star finder to agree. Then move the star disk ahead one hour to give the positions for the time of sunrise. Now look along the "ecliptic" on the star disk, where the sun's position is marked for various dates, and read the date which lies on the eastern horizon. As an example, if you had been out on the morning of June 22, you would have seen Aldebaran just above the horizon an hour before sunrise. Adjusting the star disk to that position and then moving it ahead an hour to bring the sun to the horizon, you find the date, June 22 (give or take a few days), marked on the zodiac.

Table 2 lists the dates on which other bright stars rise *with* the sun and one hour *before* the sun. (Ordinarily, you will not see a star unless it rises almost a full hour before the sun.) Such tables were used by the ancient astronomers to keep track of the seasons.

The date may also be determined by observing the stars after sunset. As before, set the star finder to agree with the observed positions of the stars, but now shift the star disk *back* by the amount of time elapsed since sunset, and read the date where the zodiac crosses the western horizon. (In all of this you must, of course, use the true horizontal direction rather than a horizon obstructed by a mountain.)

TABLE 2
STARS THAT RISE WITH THE SUN ON VARIOUS DATES

STAR OR GROUP	CONSTELLATION	RISES WITH SUN (INVISIBLE)	RISES ONE HOUR BEFORE SUN
Alpha and Beta	Capricornus	Jan. 15	Feb. 7
Alpheratz	Pegasus	Feb. 1	Mar. 1
Circlet	Pisces	Feb. 20	Mar. 20
	Triangulum	Mar. 18	Apr. 16
Pleiades	Taurus	May 16	June 3
Aldebaran	Taurus	June 7	June 22
Betelgeuse	Orion	July 2	July 16
Pollux	Gemini	July 10	July 25
Procyon	Canis Minor	July 27	Aug. 9
Sirius	Canis Major	Aug. 4	Aug. 15
Regulus	Leo	Aug. 21	Sept. 2
Denebola	Leo	Sept. 10	Sept. 22
Arcturus	Boötes	Oct. 7	Oct. 20
Spica	Virgo	Oct. 17	Oct. 29
Alpha	Libra	Nov. 6	Nov. 19
Albireo	Cygnus	Nov. 26	Dec. 6
Antares	Scorpius	Dec. 7	Dec. 18
Altair	Aquila	Dec. 15	Dec. 27

RECAPITULATION

In this chapter, the following uses of the star finder have been described:

GIVEN	TO FIND
1. Date	Sun time
2. Nothing	Date

Several variations on these two problems may also be handled, and you may devise your own solutions. For example, given the sun time, you may find the date by noting the position of the stars. (This is Problem 1 in reverse.)

With the star finder you may also predict the times of sunrise and sunset for any day of the year. This is discussed in the next chapter.

Sunset and Sunrise

TIMES OF SUNSET AND SUNRISE

At the time of the equinoxes (around March 21 and September 21) the sun is on the equator and it rises and sets at about six o'clock, local sun time, no matter where you are in the world. In other seasons, the times of sunset and sunrise depend on your latitude as well as on the date.

     Times of sunset and sunrise in a particular city may often be found with the weather forecast in a local newspaper. These times vary with your location, and Tables 3a and 3b, giving times for the *center* of time zones anywhere in the world at various latitudes, may be quite wrong if you are somewhere else, but you may derive corrections for your location by looking outside.

PREDICTING SUNSET AND SUNRISE WITH THE STAR FINDER

For any given date, the times of sunset and sunrise for the center of your time zone and at a latitude of 40° N or 30° S may be found quite easily with the star finder. (Tables 3a and 3b may be used as a check.) On the scale of dates running along the zodiac, find the sun's position for the date of interest. Set this point at the eastern horizon (for sunrise) or the western horizon (sunset), and then locate the date on the outer scale of the star disk. Read the time adjacent to the date.

A PECULIAR FEATURE OF SUNSET AND SUNRISE TIMES

One would think that the shortest day would coincide with the latest sunrise and the earliest sunset; conversely, the longest day might be expected to coincide with the earliest sunrise and the latest sunset. But that is not the way it works, as can be seen by glancing at Tables 3a and 3b. For example, in the Southern Hemisphere, the shortest day is around June 21, but the latest sunrise occurs a week earlier, while the earliest sunset is a week later. A similar, but slightly different, shift occurs in the Northern Hemisphere. Another peculiarity is that the sunrises and sunsets on the equator do not always occur at 6 a.m. and 6 p.m.

This behavior is a result of the way we conventionally measure time. Our clocks are adjusted to the average motion of the sun, and because the Earth's orbit is not circular, the sun appears to move more quickly eastward among the stars in winter than in summer. This makes our clocks appear to lag behind the sun in December, January, and February and to move ahead in July, August, and September. This contributes a part of the peculiarity. The remainder is caused by the sun's annual north and south motion, which slows its eastward motion among the stars at the time of the equinoxes, permitting our clocks to move ahead slightly. The combination of these effects, known as the "equation of time," can be seen by scanning the sunrise times in Table 3a. It amounts to about 16 minutes, at most.

TABLE 3a

APPROXIMATE TIMES OF SUNRISE

LATITUDE		+50°	+40°	+20°	0°	−20°	−40°	−50°
DATE								
Dec.	31	7:59	7:22	6:35	5:59	5:26	4:35	3:56
Jan.	15	7:53	7:20	6:38	6:06	5:34	4:49	4:12
	30	7:37	7:11	6:36	6:10	5:43	5:06	4:38
Feb.	14	7:13	6:55	6:30	6:11	5:51	5:24	5:04
Mar.	1	6:44	6:34	6:20	6:09	6:00	5:45	5:34
	16	6:12	6:11	6:08	6:06	6:02	5:57	5:54
	31	5:40	5:46	5:55	6:01	6:06	6:13	6:18
Apr.	15	5:08	5:23	5:42	5:57	6:11	6:28	6:41
	30	4:39	5:02	5:32	5:54	6:16	6:44	7:04
May	15	4:15	4:45	5:24	5:53	6:22	6:59	7:27
	30	3:58	4:34	5:20	5:54	6:27	7:10	7:45
June	14	3:50	4:30	5:20	5:57	6:32	7:19	7:57
	29	3:53	4:34	5:23	6:00	6:36	7:23	8:00
July	14	4:06	4:36	5:25	6:01	6:35	7:19	7:53
	29	4:25	4:55	5:34	6:03	6:31	7:10	7:36
Aug.	13	4:46	5:09	5:39	6:02	6:24	6:52	7:13
	28	5:08	5:24	5:43	5:58	6:13	6:30	6:44
Sept.	12	5:31	5:38	5:47	5:53	6:01	6:04	6:10
	27	5:53	5:52	5:50	5:48	5:43	5:40	5:38
Oct.	12	6:17	6:07	5:54	5:43	5:32	5:17	5:05
	27	6:41	6:23	5:59	5:41	5:22	4:56	4:36
Nov.	11	7:06	6:40	6:06	5:41	5:15	4:40	4:12
	26	7:29	6:57	6:15	5:44	5:11	4:27	3:52
Dec.	11	7:48	7:12	6:25	5:50	5:14	4:24	3:44
	26	7:58	7:20	6:33	5:57	5:20	4:30	3:49

TABLE 3b
APPROXIMATE TIMES OF SUNSET

LATITUDE		+50°	+40°	+20°	0°	−20°	−40°	−50°
DATE								
Dec.	31	16:08	16:44	17:31	18:07	18:43	19:32	20:12
Jan.	15	16:26	16:59	17:41	18:13	18:46	19:34	20:13
	30	16:51	17:17	17:51	18:17	18:44	19:20	19:48
Feb.	14	17:16	17:34	17:59	18:18	18:37	19:03	19:23
Mar.	1	17:42	17:52	18:05	18:16	18:25	18:40	18:50
	16	18:06	18:08	18:10	18:12	18:14	18:19	18:23
	31	18:30	18:23	18:14	18:08	18:00	17:58	18:10
Apr.	15	18:53	18:38	18:18	18:08	17:49	17:31	17:18
	30	19:17	18:53	18:23	18:01	17:39	17:10	16:46
May	15	19:39	19:08	18:29	18:00	17:32	16:54	16:25
	30	19:58	19:21	18:35	18:01	17:27	16:43	16:09
June	14	20:01	19:30	18:40	18:04	17:28	16:40	16:03
	29	20:13	19:33	18:43	18:07	17:31	16:44	16:07
July	14	20:05	19:29	18:43	18:09	17:38	16:54	16:21
	29	19:47	19:17	18:39	18:10	17:41	17:06	16:38
Aug.	13	19:23	19:00	18:30	18:08	17:47	17:20	16:59
	28	18:53	18:38	18:19	18:05	17:50	17:33	17:19
Sept.	12	18:21	18:14	18:06	18:00	17:56	17:47	17:43
	27	17:48	17:49	17:52	17:54	17:58	18:02	18:05
Oct.	12	17:16	17:26	17:39	17:50	18:02	18:17	18:30
	27	16:46	17:04	17:29	17:47	18:17	18:33	18:53
Nov.	11	16:22	16:48	17:22	17:48	18:18	18:50	19:19
	26	16:05	16:37	17:19	17:51	18:23	19:07	19:42
Dec.	11	15:58	16:35	17:22	17:57	18:33	19:22	20:02
	26	16:03	16:41	17:28	18:04	18:41	19:31	20:11

DOUBLING YOUR SUNSETS

Dennis Rawlins (in an article in the *American Journal of Physics,* February, 1979) has pointed out that it is easy to see the sunset more than once in an evening. The trick is to lie on the ground where a sharp western horizon is far away—the seashore is ideal, but the plains will do. Then, just as the last bright point of sunlight vanishes, leap up and look again; or, better yet, dash up a hill. (If there is no hill, you can compare your time of sunset, seen while lying on the ground, with the time seen by a companion in a tower or in a tall building.) The higher

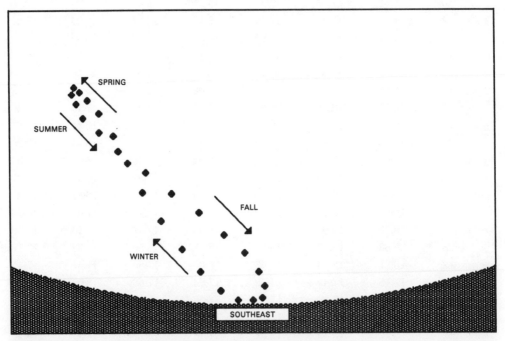

Figure 22. Looking southeast at 7:30 a.m. from latitude 40° N. Each dot represents the early-morning position of the sun at two-week intervals around the year. The sun is lowest in December, at the transition between fall and winter, indicating that the sunrise was latest at that time of year. As winter gives way to spring, the sun moves to the left (north) and is higher in the sky by 7:30 each morning. This track (indicated by the arrows) is the so-called "analemma" showing the relation between the clock and the position of the sun through the year. A splendid photographic realization of this sunrise analemma can be found in Sky and Telescope *magazine for June 1979.*

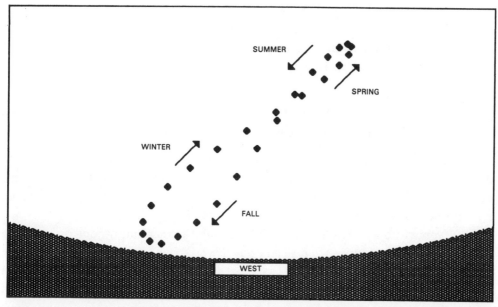

Figure 23. Sunset analemma for latitude 40° N. This figure is similar to Figure 22, showing the position of the sun in the western sky at 4:20 p.m. at two-week intervals around the year. Compare with Figure 22. Note that the sun moves northward and is higher in the sky each afternoon as winter gives way to spring. Arrows indicate the sun's path along the analemma.

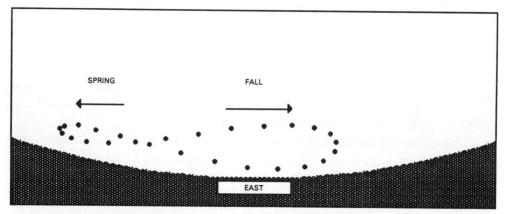

Figure 24. Sunset analemma on the equator (latitude 0°). Similar to Figures 22 and 23. At the equator, the seasonal motion is mostly along the horizon, so although the position of sunset moves north and south, the time of sunset changes very little in the course of the year.

you are, the later is the sunset, because the Earth is round. (The effect is the same as the "dip of the horizon," well known to celestial navigators.)

Even if you only jump up about 2 meters (6 feet), the second sunset will occur ten or twenty seconds after the first.

GUESSING THE TIME REMAINING
UNTIL SUNRISE AND SUNSET

Morning twilight begins when the sun is 12° to 15° below the horizon and its rays strike the upper layers of the atmosphere. The interval between this moment and the time of actual sunrise will vary with the season and your latitude, but one hour is a useful estimate for the middle latitudes.

Even without a watch, it is possible to make a surprisingly good guess of the time remaining until sunset—on a clear day. If you spread your thumb and fingers, and then extend your arm, the distance between the tip of your thumb and the tip of your index finger will be approximately 15°, the sun's motion in one hour. (Not all hands are the same, so you should develop a technique that makes your hand extend one twenty-fourth of a full circle.) Using your extended hand, measure the distance from the sun to the point on the horizon where the sun will set. Doing this, you can guess the corresponding time interval to within a quarter-hour with a little practice.

TWILIGHT COLORS

As far as colors go, sunrise is just sunset in reverse, so I will not distinguish between them. (Also, moonrise and moonset would appear just as colorful as sunset if our eyes were more sensitive to faint light.)

Sunset colors fade when the sun has descended too far to illuminate the atmospheric clouds and dust, so the duration of these added colors is determined by two factors: the varying height of the sun and the height of clouds and dust in the air.

Look eastward immediately after sunset and you will see the horizon darken as the broad, indistinct shadow of the Earth climbs rapidly up the sky, leaving the clouds and lower air in darkness. (This is the only time of the day that the horizon is darker than the sky overhead. At all other times—even at night—the horizon is brighter than the sky overhead.)

Thirty minutes later, you will see a pink glow in the western sky halfway toward the zenith. This is sunlight scattered by dust in a narrow layer at a height of forty miles.

THE SHAPE AND SIZE OF THE SETTING SUN

The setting sun is highly flattened because the Earth's atmosphere raises the lower portion of the sun more than the upper portion. This *refraction* is sufficient to keep the sun above the horizon two minutes after it would have set.

Figure 25 shows the effects of atmospheric refraction near sunset. The dotted lines indicate the true sun and the horizon, while the apparent image, as seen through the atmosphere, is shown as an oval. In the right-hand image, the true sun is entirely below the horizon, while we see it to be entirely above the

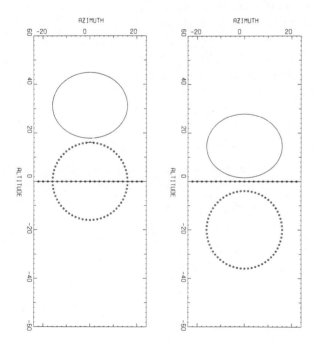

Figure 25. The shape of the setting sun is affected by the Earth's atmosphere. The true sun (dotted circles) and its refracted image (ovals) are shown at two moments just before apparent sunset. The ovals are computed taking into account the influence of the Earth's atmosphere at sea level on a normal day. In the right-hand figure, the true sun is entirely below the horizon before the apparent sun has begun to set. Azimuth and altitude are indicated in minutes of arc (¹/₆₀°).

horizon. (On Venus, refraction would carry sunlight all around the planet. If it were not for clouds, the sun would appear never to set; it would appear to spread all around the horizon.) Like the moon, the sun appears very large when it is near the horizon, but this must be a psychological effect, because measurements show there is no such magnification.

THE MIDNIGHT SUNS

Those who live beyond the Arctic and Antarctic circles (66½° from the equator) will see the midnight sun during a portion of the summer. The closer to the poles, the longer is the interval; there is a corresponding interval without sunlight during winter. The following table lists the intervals of the midnight sun for various latitudes in the Northern Hemisphere.

LATITUDE (N)	INTERVALS OF MIDNIGHT SUN
67°	June 6–July 9
71°	May 15–July 31
75°	Apr. 30–Aug. 14
79°	Apr. 18–Aug. 27
83°	Apr. 7–Sept. 7

For those in the Southern Hemisphere, the seasons of midnight sun are as follows:

LATITUDE (S)	INTERVALS OF MIDNIGHT SUN
67°	Dec. 6–Jan. 6
71°	Nov. 15–Jan. 27
75°	Nov. 1–Feb. 10
79°	Oct. 21–Feb. 22
83°	Oct. 10–Mar. 4

6
Eclipses

LUNAR ECLIPSES

With luck, you may see several eclipses of the moon each year, no matter where you are. These eclipses occur when the moon enters the Earth's shadow, which consists of two cones pointing away from the sun. One, the narrow *umbra,* converges and vanishes at a distance of one million miles, well beyond the moon. The other, the broad *penumbra,* diverges and extends endlessly. Within the umbra, the sun's face is completely hidden from the moon; within the penumbra, it is partially hidden. (See Figure 26.)

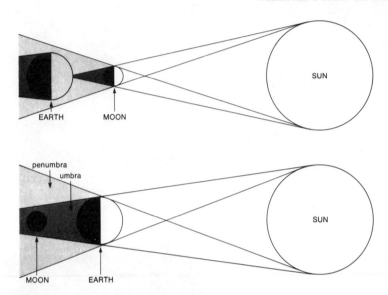

Figure 26. Schematic diagrams of an eclipse of the sun (upper) and a total eclipse of the moon (lower). The Earth's shadow (and the moon's) consists of two portions, the dark inner umbra and the penumbra. A traveler in the penumbral region would see the sun partially eclipsed; in the umbra the sun appears totally eclipsed.

A lunar eclipse commences with the passage of the Earth's faint and indistinct penumbral shadow over the face of the moon. This phase of the eclipse is difficult to see, but after an hour or so the edge of the umbral shadow strikes the moon's face. The umbral shadow is dark and slightly reddish; the penumbral shadow is bright and silvery by comparison. At totality the moon will nearly vanish, but in most eclipses a remnant of light remains—light that has passed through the atmosphere of the Earth. (During several recent eclipses, astronomers have used world-wide cloud data to show that clouds in our atmosphere affect the brightness of the eclipsed moon.)

SOLAR ECLIPSES

The moon also casts umbral and penumbral shadows. During a partial eclipse of the sun, we stand in the penumbral shadow of the moon. The umbral shadow of the moon is about one-quarter as long as the Earth's, because the moon's diameter is one-quarter the Earth's, and the most amazing coincidence of the solar system is that the moon's umbral shadow reaches precisely to the Earth's surface. To express this coincidence in slightly different terms, the moon has precisely the correct size to cover the face of the sun as seen from the Earth. (And, to say it in a third way, the moon's distance is 1/400 the sun's distance and its true size is 1/400 the sun's true size.)

As a result of this coincidence, total solar eclipses are spectacular and they may be seen only from a very narrow band of the Earth's surface.

The sight of a total eclipse of the sun will repay a few hundred miles' travel, even for the person who does nothing but gawk. The eclipsed sun is a black hole in the sky, surrounded by the glowing corona of the sun's atmosphere. Stars appear, and the horizon seems engulfed by an immense forest fire. For me, the most amazing feature of an eclipse is its silence. I expect the grinding of machinery or a few claps of thunder, but I only hear the barking of dogs and the evening songs of confused birds. Until you have seen a total eclipse, it is difficult to imagine how it differs from a partial eclipse and from an eclipse of the moon.

Figure 27. Central paths of solar eclipses between 1985 and 1995. The heavy lines indicate regions of total eclipse; lighter lines indicate regions of annular eclipse in which the moon's disc is not large enough to cover the sun completely. (Diagram by Fred Espenak, courtesy Sky & Telescope.*)*

WHERE TO GO TO SEE AN ECLIPSE

Tracks of the sun's umbral shadow during the next five years are shown in Figure 27. On July 11, 1991, you should plan to be on the island of Hawaii, in Baja California, or in Mexico. There will be a splendid total eclipse of the sun that day. A detailed map of the path of totality can be found in *Sky & Telescope* magazine* for February 1989, page 134.

THE SEASONS OF ECLIPSES

If the moon followed precisely the sun's path around the sky, we would see a solar eclipse every month at new moon and a lunar eclipse at full moon, but the 5° tilt of the moon's orbit prevents this, as is indicated in Figure 28. The moon's

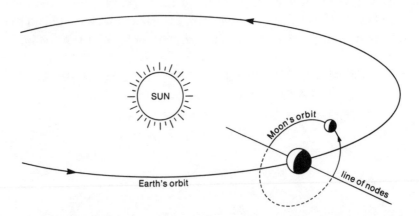

Figure 28. Diagram illustrating why eclipses occur only at two seasons of the year. The moon's orbit is tilted 5° from the Earth's orbit, and the two orbital planes intersect along the "lines of nodes." Eclipses of the sun and moon can only occur when the Earth's orbital motion carries it to the places where the line of nodes points directly at the sun. These two places are opposite sides of the orbit so eclipses occur at two times a year, six months apart. (A slow movement of the line of nodes causes the eclipses to occur at slightly different times each year.)

---

*This magazine, published in Cambridge, Massachusetts, is available in many public libraries.

monthly track crosses the sun's path at two points called the *nodes,* and an eclipse can occur only when the sun is near one of them. Because the sun requires six months to move from one node to the other, eclipses occur at intervals of about six months. In 1986, for example, eclipses occurred in April and October. During the following years, eclipses will occur at different times; the dates are given at the end of the book.

The moon's orbit rotates around the ecliptic, and the nodes move westward, making a complete cycle in eighteen years. Thus, eclipses occur several weeks earlier in succeeding years. (The eighteen-year cycle is called the Saros, and it was known to the ancients.)

PHOTOGRAPHY OF ECLIPSES AND OTHER EVENTS

A great deal happens in a short time during a solar eclipse, and if you make a photographic record you will probably see many things you missed during the actual eclipse. (Of course, you also run the danger of having to fuss with your camera at the height of the eclipse when everyone else is calmly admiring the spectacle.) I find color transparency film far more satisfactory than black and white, particularly when the pictures are projected onto a large screen. And movies are fascinating.

During the few minutes before and after totality, the sun's crescent appears deceptively faint and harmless, but it is nearly as dangerous as the full sun. Thus it is not difficult to burn a hole in your retina by looking at the partially eclipsed sun, either with the naked eye or through the viewfinder of your camera. Also, the heat of the sunlight can burn a hole in your camera shutter or cause it to warp, so you must use filters.

A safe filter for your eyes may be made from two thicknesses of heavily exposed and fully developed photographic film. Polaroids and gelatin filters are not safe, because they transmit infrared radiation that may be damaging. For your camera, a No. 5 neutral-density filter is adequate. These filters should be removed during totality. There is no danger in looking at the totally eclipsed sun, but don't be caught looking at the emerging crescent after totality has passed.

The focal length of your camera lens will determine the size of the sun's image. Divide the focal length by 100 to determine the size. For example, a

TABLE 4
SOLAR ECLIPSE PHOTOGRAPHY
APPROXIMATE EXPOSURES FOR STILL AND MOVIE CAMERAS

ASA SPEED		PARTIAL PHASES		TOTALITY (PROMI- NENCES)		TOTALITY (INNER CORONA)		TOTALITY (OUTER CORONA)	
		STILL	MOVIE	STILL	MOVIE	STILL	MOVIE	STILL	MOVIE
25–32	Lens Opening	f/5.6	f/11	f/4.5	f/8	f/4.5	f/2.8	f/4.5	f/1.4
	ND Filter	5.00	5.00	none		none		none	
	Time (seconds)	1/100	16 FPS	1/100	16 FPS	1/10	16 FPS	1/2	16 FPS
40–50	Lens Opening	f/6.3	f/13	f/5.6	f/11	f/5.6	f/3.5	f/5.6	f/1.9
	ND Filter	5.00	5.00	none		none		none	
	Time (seconds)	1/100	16 FPS	1/100	16 FPS	1/10	16 FPS	1/2	16 FPS
64	Lens Opening	f/8	f/16	f/6.3	f/13	f/6.3	f/4	f/6.3	f/2
	ND Filter	5.00	5.00	none		none		none	
	Time (seconds)	1/100	16 FPS	1/100	16 FPS	1/10	16 FPS	1/2	16 FPS
125–160	Lens Opening	f/11	f/22	f/8	f/16	f/8	f/4.5	f/8	f/2
	ND Filter	5.00	5.00	none		none		none	
	Time (seconds)	1/100	16 FPS	1/100	16 FPS	1/10	16 FPS	1/2	16 FPS
200–250	Lens Opening	f/16	f/9.5	f/11	f/22	f/11	f/6.3	f/11	f/2.8
	ND Filter	5.00	6.00	none		none		none	
	Time (seconds)	1/100	16 FPS	1/100	16 FPS	1/10	16 FPS	1/2	16 FPS
400–650	Lens Opening	f/22	f/11	f/16	f/11	f/16	f/9.5	f/16	f/4
	ND Filter	5.00	6.00	none	1.00	none		none	
	Time (seconds)	1/100	16 FPS	1/100	16 FPS	1/10	16 FPS	1/2	16 FPS
1250	Lens Opening	f/32	f/16	f/22	f/16	f/22	f/13	f/22	f/5.6
	ND Filter	5.00	6.00	none	1.00	none		none	
	Time (seconds)	1/100	16 FPS	1/100	16 FPS	1/10	16 FPS	1/2	16 FPS

FPS = Frames Per Second.

four-inch lens will produce an image on the film 4/100 inches in diameter. This is the thickness of a dime. When a transparency is projected onto a screen with a magnification of 100×, the resulting image of the sun will have a diameter equal to the focal length of the camera.

During the partial phases, the sun should be photographed with the longest focal length available, and you should also notice the peculiar crescent-shaped shadows produced by light filtering through the leaves of trees.

During totality, a short focal length lens can capture an interesting general view of the eclipse and will reveal the glowing sky beyond the limits of the moon's shadow. With a moderate telephoto lens you can catch the general shape of the sun's corona, a pale glowing atmosphere that extends many times the diameter of the sun. With an extreme telephoto, you will see details of the coronal stream-ers, and you may be able to catch Baily's beads, spots of sunlight shining through valleys on the moon during the few seconds before and after totality.

Vary your exposures and shoot lots of film. It is difficult to make precise predictions of the best exposure for each set of conditions, but the guidelines in Table 4, developed by the Eastman Kodak Company, give representative values based on the experience of numerous photographers. There are several good sources of information on photographing a variety of objects, such as meteors and comets, and the following magazines often carry helpful articles:

Sky & Telescope, 49 Bay State Road, Cambridge, MA 02238

Astronomy, PO Box 92788, Milwaukee, WI 53202

The Astrograph, PO Box 2283, Arlington, VA 22202

Catching
the Unpredictable

SUNSPOTS

If you use the following method, sunspots are quite easy to see. Focus a pair of binoculars or a telescope on an object about forty feet away. Then support the binoculars against a railing or a tree trunk, place a sheet of white paper two feet behind the eyepiece, and point the binoculars toward the sun. (For heaven's sake, DON'T LOOK THROUGH THEM.) By adjusting the focus and moving the paper toward and away from the eyepiece, you will be able to throw a sharp image of the sun onto the paper. An image two inches across will make the sunspots fairly easy to see—if there are any.

Many sunspots are larger than the Earth, but with binoculars they look like fly specks. Move the paper and keep looking. You will probably find two or three.

Sunspots usually persist for at least a week, and if you watch for a few days you will be able to see them move with the rotation of the sun. In two weeks a spot will move entirely across the sun's face.

Sunspots are areas which have been cooled by magnetic fields in the sun's atmosphere, and they are also the location of the fierce magnetic storms—"flares"—that shoot solar atoms toward the Earth and cause the northern lights.

AURORAE BOREALIS AND AURORAE AUSTRALIS

The high layers of the atmosphere often glow brightly as atoms from the sun enter the Earth's magnetic field.

Aurorae are not connected with the seasons, but they are more often seen during the winter because the nights are longer and the air tends to be less hazy. Bright ones show patches of red or green, and sometimes both. These colors, like those of an electric sign, are produced by colliding atoms. Pulsations of brightness are not unusual.

Aurorae are rarely seen near the equator. The region of greatest activity in the Northern Hemisphere is a lopsided ring passing over Canada, Alaska, Siberia, and Scandinavia. In this zone, aurorae can be seen on almost every clear, moonless night of the year. In the Southern Hemisphere, the most intense aurorae occur over the ocean, in an irregular ring surrounding Antarctica.

WHERE TO HUNT THE RAINBOW

Raindrops and sunlight can also produce colors when they are mixed in the right part of the sky. (It is not necessary to have raindrops falling on your head.) Actually there are two bows of color, and the strongest forms a circle of radius 42° around the direction opposite the sun. The weaker bow lies 9° outside, and its colors are reversed. (This reversal occurs because the sunlight bounces twice inside the drop rather than once, which also accounts for the faintness of the secondary bow, because a great deal of light is lost on each bounce.)

You must always turn your back on the sun to see a rainbow. If the sun is nearly setting, the center of the bow will lie just below the opposite horizon, and the bow will stand high in the sky. When the sun is high overhead, you must look farther down to see the rainbow, and you may see one in a garden sprinkler or the spray of a boat. (Rainbows should also be visible from the top of a mountain when the sun is high.)

HALOES AND SUN DOGS

Ice crystals floating in the air can also produce circular arcs of light, although their colors are much less striking than those of the rainbow. At night, a circular halo about the moon reveals a thin layer of cirrus clouds, and it often portends a change for the worse in the weather.

Many other forms of haloes may be seen in sunlight (Figure 29). A halo of 22° radius centered on the sun is not uncommon, and in late afternoon it is often possible to see diffuse spots of faintly colored light on either side of the sun at a distance of 22°. These are the "sun dogs." And there are other, less common forms produced by ice crystals of various shapes falling through the air in various positions. Although they are indistinct, these arcs and haloes may be photographed. Color film is preferable.

COMETS

Every few years a comet passes near the sun and becomes visible to the naked eye for several weeks. The head of a comet is composed of a "snowball" a few miles in diameter surrounded by a diffuse halo. The tail of a comet is composed of gas and dust released from the nucleus by the heat of sunlight and propelled outward by sunlight and solar atoms. Some comets have several tails, each ejected from a different portion of the nucleus or composed of different types of particles.

In 1759, Halley's Comet became the first whose return had been predicted, and its orbit has been traced back to an ancient observation in 256 B.C. The comet's orbital period fluctuates (largely because of its occasional close approaches to the Earth) between 70 and 79 years—presently standing at 76 years. The appearance of 12 B.C. was seen in Rome and China, and its great brilliance in 1301 inspired the painter Giotto to depict it as having been the "Star of Bethlehem."

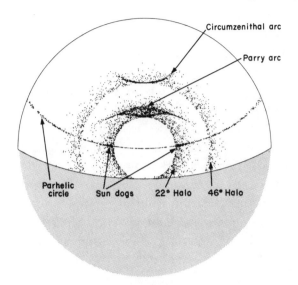

Figure 29. Haloes and sun dogs. A computer simulation of haloes and arcs produced by refraction and reflection of sunlight or moonlight in ice crystals floating in the air. Note the two elongated "sun dogs" on the parhelic circle, which are among the more common phenomena. The sizes of the haloes depend on the refractive properties of ice and on the six-sided shape of the crystals, but variations in atmospheric conditions and the height of the sun will emphasize some haloes at the expense of others. In constructing this diagram, the sun was assumed to be 20° above the horizon and the paths of many hundreds of photons from the light source were traced to an observer on the ground. (Adapted from Robert Greenler, Rainbows, Haloes, and Glories. *New York: Cambridge University Press, 1980.)*

METEORS

The flash of a meteor is caused by a fragment, often no larger than a fingernail, descending through the atmosphere at speeds of ten to fifty miles per second. We see them at heights of about fifty miles, and they seldom reach the ground.

Meteors come in two varieties: "sporadic" and "shower." On every dark night of the year, it is possible to see a sporadic, or random, meteor every few minutes. There is no telling where the next will appear, because they are scattered through the solar system and presumably are fragments left over from the formation of the planets. Occasionally a very large fragment will produce a "fireball," remaining visible for hundreds of miles and crashing to earth as a meteorite.

Meteor "showers" are produced by swarms of cometary debris that follow their parents about the sun. Every comet produces such a swarm, but we encounter only a few of them. When we do, the meteors appear to fan out from a single point in the sky. This is the "radiant," and the shower is named for the constellation or star near that point. On the night of a shower, hundreds of meteors may be seen in a few hours. Table 5 lists the best showers. They appear on the same date each year, because their orbits are fixed in the solar system.

Little is gained by looking for meteors with binoculars or telescopes because such devices restrict your field of view. Photography is not difficult. Leave the camera open for a half-hour or so. Moonlight is a definite hindrance (and will make such photography impossible), so it is best to look for meteors in a moonless sky.

TABLE 5
THE MOST INTENSE METEOR SHOWERS

NAME	DATES	MAXIMUM HOURLY RATE	ASSOCIATED COMET
Quadrantids	Jan. 3	50	?
Eta Aquarids	May 5+4	20	Halley
Delta Aquarids	July 28+3	20	?
Perseids	Aug. 12+2	50	1862 III
Draconids	Oct. 10	Variable	Giacobini-Zinner
Orionids	Oct. 21+3	20	Halley
Leonids	Nov. 17+3	10	Temple
Geminids	Dec. 12+2	50	?
Ursids	Dec. 22+3	15	Tuttle

NORTHEAST

Figure 30. Schematic diagram of the region of Perseus in the evening of August 11–12, showing several Perseid meteors radiating from the constellation. Members of meteor showers, such as the Perseids, move together through space, and they appear to diverge from a distant point when they burn in the Earth's atmosphere.

Some Odds and Ends

THE TOTAL NUMBER OF VISIBLE STARS

On the entire celestial sphere there are about 5,000 stars brighter than sixth magnitude, the limit for average eyesight, and in an open space on a clear night you can see approximately 2,000. The visible stars give only one-fifth of the total light of the stars; the remainder is contributed by stars too faint to be seen individually.

And starlight itself contributes less than one-sixth of the total light of the sky. Even on the darkest night, faint aurorae and light scattered by dust among the planets give five times more light than the stars.

Binoculars with two-inch (50 mm.) lenses will permit you to see about

235,000 stars on the celestial sphere—nearly fifty times as many as the naked eye. And with a six-inch telescope, you would be able to count 2,600,000. The largest telescope in the world would reveal more than a billion stars.

THE CENTER OF OUR GALAXY

Our galaxy contains two dozen stars for every human, or about 100 billion. Only one percent can be photographed individually even with the largest telescopes; the remainder produce the diffuse band of the Milky Way. Many stars in our galaxy are hidden by clouds of interstellar dust, and these clouds give the Milky Way a ragged and irregular appearance.

The brightest and broadest portion of the Milky Way lies in Sagittarius, and it may be seen low in the south during summer evenings in the Northern Hemisphere, or high overhead during winter in the Southern Hemisphere. This is the center of our galaxy.

Determining the precise size of our galaxy has been a difficult task, and one of the best methods is the one used by Harlow Shapley in 1916. He measured brightnesses of immense clusters of stars swarming about the center, and when corrections are made for the obscuration by dust, the result is 25,000 light-years.

THE MAGNITUDES AND BRIGHTNESSES OF STARS

The ancients divided the visible stars into six steps of brightness, called *magnitudes.* The twenty brightest stars were placed in the first magnitude, and the faintest were placed in the sixth. The steps were uniform, so stars of second magnitude, for example, appeared to be halfway between those of the first and third.

Experimenters of the nineteenth century discovered that these magnitude steps correspond to equal *ratios* of brightness, and the ratio between the ancient classes of first and second magnitude is very nearly the same as the ratio between the brightness of second- and third-magnitude stars, and so on. This rule is the basis for the modern definition of stellar magnitudes, which states that a difference of one magnitude corresponds to a brightness ratio of 2.512. This number was chosen so a difference of five magnitudes would correspond precisely to a ratio of 100 in brightness. Table 6 gives the relative brightnesses of stars of different magnitudes, and Figure 31 indicates the magnitudes of the brighter stars of the Pleiades.

TABLE 6
STELLAR MAGNITUDES AND BRIGHTNESSES
RELATIVE TO THE FAINTEST NAKED-EYE STARS

MAGNITUDE	RELATIVE BRIGHTNESS	EXAMPLE
–1	631	Canopus
0	251	Vega
1	100	Spica
2	39.8	Castor
3	14.8	Cor Caroli
4	6.31	Alcor
5	2.51	
6	1.00	Faintest Naked-Eye Stars
7	0.398	
8	0.158	

Although stars of the sixth magnitude are the faintest that can normally be seen with the naked eye on a dark night, the magnitudes can be extended further with telescopes and cameras. (An eleventh-magnitude star is 100 times fainter than a sixth-magnitude star, and a sixteenth-magnitude star is fainter by another factor 100. The faintest stars that have been photographed are 4 million times fainter than the limit of the naked eye.)

Table 7 gives the total number of stars brighter than each magnitude. For example, of all the stars in the sky, 150 are brighter than third magnitude.

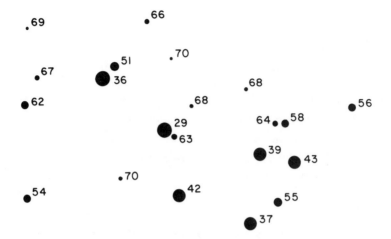

Figure 31. Stars of the Pleiades cluster ("The Seven Sisters") brighter than the seventh magnitude. This diagram will permit you to test the visibility of faint stars. Each star is labeled with its magnitude in visual light, the decimal point being omitted. (Thus, "29" indicates magnitude 2.9.) On a dark night with a clear sky, the average eye can see stars to the sixth magnitude. This cluster lies in the constellation Taurus, and it is indicated on the star finder.

TABLE 7

COUNTS OF THE STARS BY MAGNITUDE

MAGNITUDE	NUMBER BRIGHTER	MAGNITUDE	NUMBER BRIGHTER
–2.0	0	5.0	1,700
–1.0	1	6.0	4,900
0.0	4	7.0	14,000
1.0	16	10.0	350,000
2.0	45		
3.0	150	15.0	37,000,000
4.0	540	20.0	1,200,000,000

THE LIMIT OF FAINTNESS IN A TELESCOPE

The larger the area of a telescope lens or mirror, the fainter the stars that may be seen. The first two columns of Table 8 list the *limiting,* or faintest, magnitude that can be seen through telescopes of different diameters.

Also, when a photographic film is placed at the focus of a telescope, transforming it into a camera, stars can be detected nearly 100 times fainter than could be seen through the same instrument. Table 8 summarizes the limiting magnitudes that can be photographed with telescopes of various sizes. (This table is

TABLE 8

LIMITING MAGNITUDES FOR REFLECTING TELESCOPES

TELESCOPE DIAMETER (INCHES)	LIMITING MAGNITUDE* CONSISTENTLY SEEN	TOTAL STARS VISIBLE ON ENTIRE SPHERE	PHOTOGRAPHIC LIMIT (f/5 MIRROR)**
Eye	6.0	5,000	
2	9.7	235,000	15.0
3	10.6	600,000	15.5
4	11.3	1,200,000	16.2
5	11.8	1,900,000	16.8
6	12.2	2,600,000	17.5
8	12.9	5,250,000	18.0
10	13.4	7,500,000	18.3
12	13.8	12,000,000	18.5
24	15.5	52,000,000	19.8
48	17.0	190,000,000	21.0
100	18.8	600,000,000	22.0
200	20.3	1,300,000,000	23.0

*A difference of 5 magnitudes gives a brightness ratio of 100.
**The limit of an f/3 mirror is one magnitude brighter.

merely representative, because not all types of telescopes will have the same limits, nor is there universal agreement among astronomers about the practical limit of a given telescope.)

COLORED STARS

Sunlight is yellowish white, and this is typical of most stars that we can see, but there are some whose color is distinctly red or blue. (I have never seen a star that looked green, but others say they have.)

The eye has difficulty with the colors of faint stars, so you should concentrate on the brightest ones, and a pair of binoculars is helpful. The tints are as vivid as the colors in a flame.

With the star finder you can locate the stars in Table 9 whose colors are noticeable. Each is among the brightest in its constellation.

TABLE 9
STAR COLORS

NAME	CONSTELLATION	COLOR
Spica	Virgo	Blue
Arcturus	Boötes	Yellow
Pollux	Gemini	Yellow
Castor	Gemini	White
Capella	Auriga	Yellow-white (sunlight)
Rigel	Orion	Blue-white
Antares	Scorpius	Red

TESTING YOUR EYES AND BINOCULARS ON DOUBLE STARS

A test of eyesight reportedly used by the Arabs is the pair of stars Mizar and Alcor, in the handle of the Big Dipper. Mizar is as bright as the North Star (magnitude 2) and its companion is one-fourth as bright. They are separated by eleven minutes of arc. (One minute of arc is one-sixtieth of a degree. The diameters of the sun and moon are thirty minutes of arc.) Most people can separate Mizar and Alcor quite easily with their naked eyes. (Mizar itself is a double star, but the separation is only 14.5 seconds of arc, so a telescope is required.)

The star α Capricornus* provides a good test of eyesight. Its components are separated by six minutes of arc. This star forms the upper right-hand tip of the crescent-shaped constellation Capricornus.

Two "stars" in Scorpius may also be seen as double with the naked eye on a clear summer night. They are listed in Table 10 and are indicated on the star finder with the symbol - • - .

TABLE 10
NAKED-EYE DOUBLE STARS

| DESIGNATION | COORDINATES | MAGNITUDES | | SEPARATION (ARC MINUTES) |
		BRIGHTER	FAINTER	
Mizar and Alcor	13ʰ22ᵐ +55°11′	2.17	4.02	11
ι Scorpii	17 44 −40 06	3.14	4.88	9
μ Scorpii	16 48 −37 57	3.09	3.64	7
α Capricornus	20 15 −12 40	3.77	4.55	6

Even the best of eyes can rarely distinguish two stars closer than three minutes of arc, so the star ε Lyrae (separation 3.5 minutes) provides a tough test. This star is near the bright star Vega (see star finder), and my sons say they can distinguish its components quite easily, although I cannot. In a five-inch telescope this star is quite a remarkable sight, because each component can be seen as a double, and this is a *quadruple* system.

*"Alpha" is the brightest star in Capricornus. Greek letters have been assigned to the brighter stars, more or less alphabetically in order of decreasing brightness. The Greek alphabet is listed at the end of this book.

Rigidly mounted binoculars will reveal many other pairs of stars, and you will probably be able to distinguish stars whose separations are greater than five minutes of arc *divided by* the magnifying power of the binoculars. In seconds of arc, this rule gives 300/(magnifying power), or about 45 seconds for 7× binoculars. If you merely hold the binoculars in your hands instead of mounting them, your limit will probably be about half as sharp, judging from my own experience.

Table 11 lists bright double stars whose components are separated by more than forty seconds of arc and have nearly equal brightness. These stars are indicated on the star finder.

TABLE 11
DOUBLE STARS VISIBLE WITH BINOCULARS

DESIGNATION	COORDINATES	COMBINED	MAGNITUDES BRIGHTER	FAINTER	SEPARATION (ARC SECONDS)	NAME
α Librae	14ʰ48ᵐ −15°50′	2.79	2.90	5.33	231	*Zubenelgenubi*
ε Lyrae	18 43 +39 37	3.83	4.50	4.68	208	
α Leonis	10 05 +12 13	1.34	1.34	7.64	176	*Regulus*
μ Boötis	15 22 +37 33	4.33	4.47	6.67	109	*Alkalurops*
16, 17 Dra	16 35 +53 01	4.65	5.20	5.64	91	
υ Draconis	17 31 +55 13	4.20	4.95	4.98	62	
ζ Lyrae	18 43 +37 32	4.06	4.29	5.87	44	
λ Cap	20 16 −12 35	3.10	3.55	4.22	376	

Table 12 lists double stars that are beyond the reach of binoculars, but that may be separated with a small telescope.

Some of the double stars in these lists are accidental pairings of stars lying at vastly different distances from the sun. However, most of the fainter and more difficult doubles are physically connected and are moving in gravitational orbits about one another, much as the planets move around the sun. In fact, the majority of stars are members of multiple systems. (No planets have been detected beyond the solar system, but several stars appear to be twirled by a dark companion.)

TABLE 12

DOUBLE STARS VISIBLE IN SMALL TELESCOPES

DESIGNATION	COORDINATES		COMBINED	MAGNITUDES		FAINTER	SEPARATION (ARC SECONDS)	NAME
	α	δ		BRIGHTER				
υ Scorpii	16ʰ09ᵐ	−19°20′	4.16	4.29		6.49	41	*Lesath*
β Cygni	19 29	+27 52	3.10	3.24		5.36	35	*Albireo*
ι Cancri	8 43	+28 57	4.09	4.20		6.61	31	
ψ Draconis	17 43	+72 11	4.58	4.90		6.07	30	
θ Serpentis	18 54	+ 4 08	4.10	4.50		5.37	23	*Alya*
ε Monocerotis	6 21	+ 4 37	4.33	4.48		6.54	13	
α Can Ven	12 54	+38 35	2.80	2.90		5.39	20	*Cor Caroli*
ζ Ursa Majoris	13 22	+55 11	2.17	2.40		3.96	14	
κ Boötis	14 12	+52 01	4.44	4.60		6.61	13	
β Scorpii	16 02	−19 40	2.76	2.90		5.06	13	*Acrab*
γ Delphini	20 44	+15 57	4.12	4.49		5.47	10	

VARIABLE STARS

Several prominent stars show variations of brightness that are easy to spot if you compare these stars with their neighbors.

A good example is β Lyrae. This "star" is actually two stars in rotation around a common center, with a period of two weeks. When the fainter star eclipses the brighter, β Lyrae fades to one-half its usual brightness and remains faint for about one day. You can see it as the star in the corner of the parallelogram of Lyra farthest from the bright star Vega. When at its brightest, β Lyrae equals its companion at the end of the parallelogram, γ Lyrae, but on some nights it will be as faint as the star in the far corner, δ Lyrae. (See Figure 32.)

Another bright eclipsing star is Algol, or β Persei. Its period is three days, and it fades to one-third its normal brightness during the eclipses, which last for several hours. (See Figure 33.)

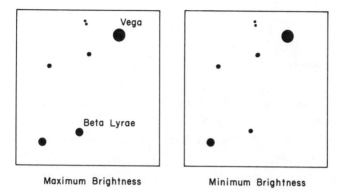

Maximum Brightness   Minimum Brightness

Figure 32. The location of the variable star Beta Lyrae. Chart showing Beta Lyrae (see text) at its normal brightness (left) and during eclipse (right). At maximum, the variable is as bright as its neighbor, while at minimum it is as bright as the star diagonally across the parallelogram.

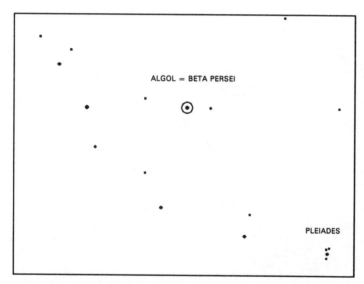

Figure 33. The region of the variable star Beta Persei, also known as Algol. (The distance from Algol to the Pleiades is about 18° on the sky. Algol is also marked on the star finder.) This is an eclipsing star whose brightness abruptly declines from magnitude 2.1 to 3.4 for a few hours every 2 days, 20 hours, 48 minutes. To catch these variations, make a drawing of the stars around Algol on every clear evening, carefully noting the relative brightnesses. Sooner or later you will catch it in an eclipse. Precise times of these eclipses can be found in the "Calendar Notes" each month in Sky and Telescope *magazine.*

In addition to eclipsing stars, there are several other classes. One star to watch is Mira, the "Wonderful." It is in the constellation Cetus, the Whale, and it reaches third or fourth magnitude at brightest, then fades to ninth magnitude about once a year. It totally vanishes for six months at a time, and its behavior is quite erratic. Mira belongs to the second class of variable stars, the *pulsators.* Its surface brightness increases and decreases as heat from the nuclear burning in the center is alternately blocked and released by the body of the star. Its surface layers also move in and out, changing the total area of the star. Pulsators represent a short stage in the life of a typical star, a stage when the star cannot remain still—somewhat like the flame of a campfire. (See Figure 34.)

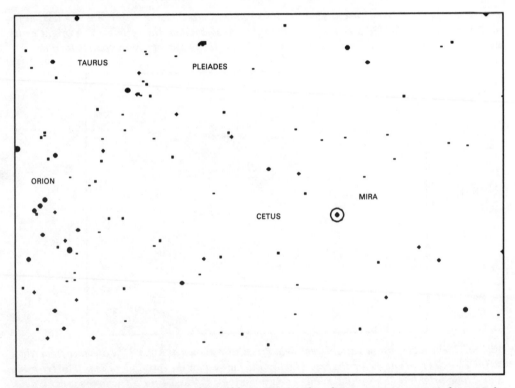

Figure 34. The region of the giant red variable star Mira. This chart covers an area of about 80° by 50°. The constellation Cetus is conveniently seen from November to February in the evening. The variable star is a pulsator whose somewhat irregular variations (see Table 15) take it from an easy naked-eye star to invisibility and back in about 10 months.

The third class of variable star, the *nova* or exploding star, has been very important for measuring the distances to other galaxies, because novae become 10,000 times brighter than the sun and can be seen at great distances. Many novae have occurred in our galaxy, and their explosions are evidently caused by the exchange of matter between two close stars; one star becomes overloaded and its surface layers erupt like a nuclear bomb. Despite the violence of the event, the stars are not destroyed.

Supernovae are the fourth class of variable star, and they become thousands of times brighter than an ordinary nova. Again, the cause is a bomblike explosion, but in these cases, the bulk of star is scattered in space, leaving a small dense residue: a neutron star. Supernovae are relatively rare; one occurs every hundred years or so in our Milky Way and at a similar rate in other galaxies like our own.

Table 13 lists the variable stars that become bright enough to be seen with the naked eye. These stars are indicated on the star finder with the symbol ⊛.

TABLE 13

BRIGHT VARIABLE STARS

NAME	POSITION		MAGNITUDE		PERIOD	TYPE
	α	ι	BRIGHTEST	FAINTEST	(DAYS)	
γ Cassiopeiae	0^h54^m	$+60°27'$	1.6	2.9	Irregular	NI
o Ceti	2 17	$-$ 3 12	3.4	9.2	331	P
β Persei	3 05	$+40\,46$	2.4	3.5	2.87	E
ϵ Aurigae	4 59	$+43\,45$	3.3	4.1	9,900	E
α Orionis	5 52	$+$ 7 24	0.5	1.1	2,070	P
L_2 Puppis	7 12	$-44\,34$	3.1	5.0	140	P
R Carinae	9 31	$-62\,34$	3.9	10.0	309	P
l Carinae	9 42	$-63\,03$	3.4	4.6	35.5	P
β Lyrae	18 48	$+33\,18$	3.4	4.1	12.91	E
κ Pavonis	18 52	$-67\,18$	3.9	4.8	9.1	P
η Aquilae	19 50	$+00\,52$	3.8	4.5	7.18	P
μ Cephei	21 42	$+58\,33$	3.7	4.7	Irregular	P
ι Cephei	22 27	$+58\,10$	3.6	4.2	5.37	P

P = Pulsator; E = Eclipsing binary; NI = Intermittent explosive activity.

The regular observing of and reporting on variable stars is a hobby of thousands of amateurs, whose work is of direct value to professional astronomers. The simplest equipment will suffice, and information on techniques, charts, and reports can be obtained from The American Association of Variable Star Observers, 187 Concord Avenue, Cambridge, Massachusetts 02138.

THE ORION NEBULA

Hanging below the "belt" of Orion is a chain of three rather indistinct "stars." The central "star" appears to be fuzzy, and it is actually a small cluster of five blue stars. With large binoculars, these stars are seen to be surrounded by a pale cloud of glowing gas. This is the Orion nebula, and the spectroscope proves that its light originates in a gas excited by the light of nearby stars. It lies within our Milky Way. (See Figure 35.)

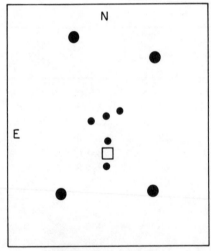

Nebula in Orion (□)

Figure 35. The location of the Great Nebula in Orion. The Great Nebula in Orion (which appears on the cover of this book) may be located with a pair of binoculars in the "sword" of three stars hanging down from the belt of Orion. The nebula looks like a slightly fuzzy star in binoculars, but a small telescope easily shows that it is a nebulosity with numerous stars embedded.

Photographs of the Orion nebula show dozens of small dark spots produced by dense clouds of dust. These clouds may contract and become stars, but a million years will have elapsed before they have become hot enough to shine like the sun.

THE ETA CARINAE NEBULA AND THE MAGELLANIC CLOUDS

The constellation Carina, in the southern Milky Way, contains a bright nebulosity that is easily seen with a pair of binoculars. It surrounds the star η Carinae, and is similar to the Great Nebula in Orion. Photographs show this nebula to have a strong reddish color, due to hydrogen emission.

A pair of objects that can only be seen well from the Southern Hemisphere are the Clouds of Magellan, marked LMC and SMC on the star finder. These are galaxies of moderate size and irregular shape; they are the Milky Way's nearest neighbors, at only one-tenth the distance of the Andromeda galaxy.

THE ZODIACAL LIGHT

This is a very faint band of light (roughly as wide as the Milky Way) which may be seen standing above the horizon among the constellations of the zodiac (hence its name). Look for it only when the sky is very dark, after evening twilight and before morning twilight. Like the planet Mercury, it appears near the sun, so the best times to see it are autumn evenings and spring mornings, although if you are at sea or in the mountains it can be seen during any season.

The zodiacal light is produced by sunlight scattered from tiny particles of cometary and meteoritic debris moving near the plane of the planets around the sun. These particles are gradually sinking toward the sun.

STAR CLUSTERS

Most stars were originally formed in large clusters containing hundreds, and occasionally thousands, of stars. The Pleiades ("Seven Sisters") is the brightest example of a star cluster in our sky, and it contains about five hundred stars, although only a handful are visible to the naked eye. Figure 31 shows the brighter members of this cluster, and the magnitudes of stars visible with binoculars are indicated. This is a very nearby example of an "open," or loose, cluster. Another example is the "double cluster" in the northern portion of the constellation Perseus, which may be picked out by the naked eye on a dark night in fall; binoculars will clearly show that it is double, but they will not reveal its individual stars—they are too far. Other examples on the star finder are the Praesepe cluster in Cancer (M44), and M7 and M41 in Scorpius and Canis Major.

If you scan the Milky Way with binoculars or a telescope, you will find dozens of faint, fuzzy patches, and many of these are open clusters too distant to show their individual stars.

Another type, the "globular" cluster, is tighter and more spherical in form. Unlike the open clusters, globular clusters avoid the plane of the Milky Way and are widely scattered throughout the galaxy, although concentrating toward its center. These differences are attributed to the fact that globular clusters were formed much earlier than open clusters, when the galaxy itself was more nearly spherical. Two of the most delightful sights in the southern sky are the globular star clusters, Omega Centauri (near the Southern Cross) and 47 Tucanae (near the Small Magellanic Cloud). These are easily seen with the naked eye on a dark night, and with a small telescope they resemble scintillating sea urchins. Containing more than 100,000 yellowish stars, they are among the oldest groups in our Milky Way. Several other globular clusters may be picked out with binoculars: M13 in Hercules, M3 in Canes Venatici between the stars Cor Caroli and Arcturus, M22 in Sagittarius, and M4 in Scorpius. These clusters are indicated with an asterisk on the star finder.

THE ANDROMEDA GALAXY (M31)

This galaxy, very much like our own, lies at a distance of 2 million light-years outside our galaxy. It is the greatest system of stars visible to the naked eye—except our own.

To find the Andromeda galaxy, start from the northeast corner of the Great Square of Pegasus. Then go two stars farther to the northeast, and then step two stars to the north. Its location is indicated by a small square on the star finder. You will see a faint oval patch of light; this is the light of 100 billion stars!

Appendixes and Index

Glossary of Astronomical Terms

Celestial Equator: The projection of the Earth's equator on the celestial sphere. This circle divides the sky into its northern and southern portions.

Celestial Pole: The point where the Earth's axis of daily rotation strikes the celestial sphere.

Celestial Sphere: An imaginary sphere against which we see the stars and on which we measure their positions.

Conjunction: Two objects are said to be *in conjunction* when they arrive at the same longitude on the ecliptic. *See* **Inferior Conjunction** and **Superior Conjunction.**

Constellation: A dot-to-dot picture in the sky. Most groups have no physical significance.

Declination: The celestial equivalent of latitude *(q.v.)*. It is measured in degrees, and its symbol is delta, δ.

Earth: I have capitalized the name of our planet in this book because I am dealing with astronomy, not soil.

Ecliptic: The band of sky in which eclipses can occur, i.e., the path of the sun. It is also the path of the planets and is tilted 23° from the equator of the Earth.

Elongation: Angular distance from the sun. Mercury is visible only within a week or two of its greatest elongations.

Equator: The great circle halfway between the North and South Poles of the Earth.

Equinox: The instant when the sun crosses the celestial equator on its path around the ecliptic. Fall equinox occurs on September 21 and spring equinox on March 21, although the times vary slightly from year to year because our calendar has leap years.

Evening Sky: The half of the sky opposite the sun.

Focal Length: The distance between a lens and the image it makes of a distant object. You can determine the focal length of your camera lens by taking it out and casting an image onto a piece of paper—or by reading the label. (One inch is 25.4 millimeters.)

Galaxy: An "island universe," or an independent system of stars. Our Milky Way is one.

Inferior Conjunction: The instant when Mercury or Venus comes between us and the sun—more precisely, when one of them arrives at the sun's longitude and is on the near side of its orbit.

Latitude: A measure of distance from the equator, expressed as the angle between the equator and a point as seen from the center of the Earth. *See* **Declination.**

Longitude: A measure of distance from Greenwich, England, expressed as an angle along the equator from the meridian of Greenwich to the meridian of the point in question. *See* **Right Ascension.**

Magnification: The ratio of angular size with and without an optical device. With 10× magnification, an object appears ten times as broad. Equivalently, it appears to be at one-tenth the distance.

Magnitude: A measure of the faintness of a star. Sixth magnitude is the faintest we can ordinarily see, and the average of the twenty brightest stars defines the first magnitude.

Meridian: An observer's meridian passes through his zenith at the celestial poles. It is his north-south line.

Meteor: A flash of light produced by a particle in the atmosphere moving so rapidly that it becomes luminous.

Meteorite: A rock that once looked like a meteor.

Morning Sky: That half of the celestial sphere containing the sun.

Nebula: A cloud of gas or dust. A nebula may be luminous if excited by a nearby star, or it may appear dark against the background of starlight. In the past, this term was also used for galaxies because they appeared nebulous.

Opposition: The instant when one of the outer planets is directly opposite the sun. Because the orbits are fairly circular, this nearly coincides with the time of closest approach to the Earth.

Planet (literally, a "wanderer"): A solid object in motion about a star. If it is very small, it is called an asteroid.

Pole: The intersection of the Earth's axis of daily rotation with the surface of the Earth or the celestial sphere.

Precession of the Equinoxes: The Earth's axis of daily rotation slowly swings about the perpendicular to the sun's path. The motion is similar to that of a spinning top and is caused by the moon's gravitational pull on the Earth's equatorial bulge. The equinoxes slide around the ecliptic in 26,000 years.

Retrograde: Backward or reversed. See the discussion of Mars's motion in Chapter 3. Jupiter and Saturn also show retrograde motions among the stars, but they are less marked.

Right Ascension: The equivalent of longitude on the celestial sphere. It is measured in hours from the spring equinox, where the ecliptic and equator intersect. The symbol for right ascension is alpha, α. One hour of right ascension is 15° of longitude.

Sky: The visible portion of the celestial sphere.

Spectrum: The color distribution of radiation from an object. Spectrum analysis permits a determination of chemical and physical composition.

Star Cluster: A group of stars within a galaxy. Some clusters contain dozens of stars; others contain millions.

Sun Dogs: Patches of light in the sky near the sun. They are produced by crystals of snow and ice high in the atmosphere.

Sunrise and Sunset: The moment when the sun's upper edge touches the imaginary horizon 90° from the zenith.

Superior Conjunction: The instant when a planet on the *far* side of the sun has the longitude of the sun. This is a time of invisibility, as is inferior conjunction.

Waning Crescent: Decreasing crescent. This occurs between full moon and new moon.

Waxing Crescent: Increasing crescent. This occurs when the moon is not waning.

Zenith: Straight up.

Zodiac: A band along the sun's annual path around the celestial sphere. *See* **Ecliptic.** The moon and planets remain in the zodiac.

The Greek Alphabet

LETTER	NAME	LETTER	NAME
α	Alpha	ν	Nu
β	Beta	ξ	Xi
γ	Gamma	o	Omicron
δ	Delta	π	Pi
ϵ	Epsilon	ρ	Rho
ζ	Zeta	σ	Sigma
η	Eta	τ	Tau
θ	Theta	υ	Upsilon
ι	Iota	ϕ	Phi
κ	Kappa	χ	Chi
λ	Lambda	ψ	Psi
μ	Mu	ω	Omega

Planetary Data

	ORBITAL PERIOD		MEAN DISTANCE FROM SUN	LEAST DISTANCE FROM EARTH	EQUATORIAL DIAMETER (MILES)	NUMBER OF KNOWN SATELLITES	MAXIMUM TEMPERATURE (FAHRENHEIT)
Mercury	88.0	days	.39	.55	3,010	0	780°
Venus	224.7	days	.72	.28	7,620	0	1,000°
Earth	365.26	days	1.00	——	7,926	1	140°
Mars	687.0	days	1.52	.38	4,220	2	75°
Jupiter	11.9	years	5.20	4	88,800	16?	−235°
Saturn	29.5	years	9.55	8	74,000	c.30	−290°
Uranus	84	years	19.20	17	29,500	5	−356°
Neptune	165	years	30.09	29	27,200	2	−360°
Pluto	248	years	39.5	29	700	1	−390° to −350°

Constellations on the Star Finder

NAME	ABBREVIATION	ENGLISH NAME	MYTHOLOGY
Andromeda	And	Andromeda	Chained woman; daughter of Cepheus and Cassiopeia.
Antlia	Ant	Air Pump	Modern.
Aquarius	Aqr	Water Carrier	
Aquila	Aql	Eagle	Armor-bearing bird of Jove.
Ara	Ara	Altar	Some say it represents one of the altars raised by Moses, others that it is the altar raised by Noah after the Deluge.
Aries	Ari	Ram	Phrixus and his sister Helle fled his stepmother on the ram; Helle fell into the sea.
Auriga	Aur	Charioteer	
Boötes	Boö	Bear Driver	
Cancer	Cnc	Crab	Banished to the sky for pinching the toe of Hercules.
Canis Major	CMa	Larger Dog	The dog of Orion.
Canis Minor	CMi	Smaller Dog	Orion's second dog.
Capricornus	Cap	Sea Goat	The goat-footed Pan; turned part fish upon plunging into the Nile to escape the monster Typhon.

NAME	ABBREVIATION	ENGLISH NAME	MYTHOLOGY
Carina	Car	Keel	The keel of the Argonauts' ship, *Navis,* of which Puppis is the stern and Vela is the sail.
Cassiopeia	Cas	Cassiopeia	Wife of Cepheus.
Centaurus	Cen	Centaur	A mythical beast consisting of a man down to the waist with the four legs of a horse.
Cepheus	Cep	Cepheus	Father of the royal family.
Cetus	Cet	Whale	Sent to devour Andromeda, Cetus turned to stone at the sight of Medusa's head in the hand of Perseus.
Corona	CrB	Crown	Crown of Ariadne, daughter of King Minos.
Corvus	Crv	Crow	Sacred bird of Phoebus Apollo, who assumed bird's shape during battle.
Crater	Crt	Cup	The cup of Apollo.
Crux	Cru	Cross	The Southern Cross.
Cygnus	Cyg	Swan	Pet of Leda, the mother of Castor and Pollux, the Twins.
Delphinus	Del	Dolphin	The sacred fish that induced Amphitrite to become the wife of Neptune.
Draco	Dra	Dragon	The snake snatched by Minerva from the giants and flung to the sky.
Eridanus	Eri	River	Flowed into the Euxine Sea where Argonauts secured the golden fleece.

NAME	ABBREVIATION	ENGLISH NAME	MYTHOLOGY
Fornax	For	Furnace	Modern.
Gemini	Gem	Twins	Sons of Leda.
Grus	Gru	Crane	Symbol of the ancient Egyptian star watchers.
Hercules	Her	Hercules	Heroic laborer.
Hydra	Hya	Sea Serpent	Kept the crow away from Apollo's cup.
Hydrus	Hyi	Serpent	
Leo	Leo	Lion	Slain by Hercules.
Lepus	Lep	Hare	Pursued by Orion and his Great Dog.
Libra	Lib	Scales	
Lupus	Lup	Wolf	
Lyra	Lyr	Lyre	Instrument of Orpheus, the musician of the Argonauts.
Monoceros	Mon	Unicorn	
Ophiuchus	Oph	Serpent Holder	Staff of Aesculapius, physician of the Argonauts.
Orion	Ori	Orion	The hunter; placed in the sky opposite the Scorpion, by whose sting he was slain.
Pavo	Pav	Peacock	Argos, builder of the ship of the Argonauts, was transformed to a peacock in the sky by the goddess Juno when she made a constellation of his ship. Symbol of immortality.

NAME	ABBREVIATION	ENGLISH NAME	MYTHOLOGY
Pegasus	Peg	Pegasus	Winged horse; born from the blood of Medusa's head, severed by Perseus.
Perseus	Per	Perseus	Rescued Andromeda, using Medusa's head to turn the Whale to stone.
Phoenix	Phe	Phoenix	Mythical bird of the Egyptians, which repeatedly consumed itself by fire and then arose from its own ashes.
Pisces	Psc	Fish	
Piscis Austrinus	PsA	Fish	Southern fish, oddly drinking water flowing from the urn of Aquarius.
Puppis	Pup	Stern	Stern of the ship sailed by Jason and the Argonauts in search of the golden fleece.
Pyxis	Pyx	Compass	
Sagittarius	Sgr	Archer	
Scorpius	Sco	Scorpion	Slayer of Orion, who sets when the Scorpion rises.
Ursa Major	UMa	Great Bear	Juno, jealous of Callisto, transformed her to a bear.
Ursa Minor	UMi	Little Bear	
Vela	Vel	Sail	*See* Carina.
Virgo	Vir	Virgin	Proserpina, daughter of Ceres, abducted by Pluto.

The Thirty Brightest Stars

NAME		MAGNITUDE	POSITION	DATE OF 9 P.M. CULMINATION
1. α CMa	Sirius	−1.47	6ʰ43ᵐ −16°39′	Feb. 15
2. α Car	Canopus	−0.73	6 21 −52 40	Feb. 10
3. α Boö	Arcturus	−0.06	14 13 +19 27	June 10
4. α Lyr	Vega	+0.04	18 35 +38 44	Aug. 10
5. α Cen		0.06	14 36 −60 38	June 15
6. β Ori	Rigel	0.08	5 12 − 8 15	Jan. 20
7. α Aur	Capella	0.09	5 13 +45 57	Jan. 20
8. α CMi	Procyon	0.34	7 37 + 5 21	Mar. 1
9. α Eri	Achernar	0.47	1 36 −57 29	Dec. 1
10. β Cen	Hadar	0.59	14 00 −60 08	June 5
11. α Aql	Altair	0.77	19 48 + 8 44	Sept. 1
12. α Ori	Betelgeuse	0.80	5 52 + 7 24	Feb. 1
13. α Tau	Aldebaran	0.86	4 33 +16 25	Jan. 15
14. α Vir	Spica	0.96	13 23 −10 54	May 25
15. α Cru		1.05	12 24 −62 49	May 10
16. α Sco	Antares	1.08	16 26 −26 19	July 10
17. β Gem	Pollux	1.15	7 42 +28 09	Mar. 1
18. α PsA	Fomalhaut	1.16	22 55 −29 53	Oct. 15
19. β Cru		1.24	12 45 −59 25	May 15
20. α Cyg	Deneb	1.26	20 40 +45 06	Sept. 15
21. α Leo	Regulus	1.35	10 06 +12 13	Apr. 9
22. ε CMa	Adhara	1.50	6 57 −28 54	Feb. 20
23. α Gem	Castor	1.58	7 31 +32 00	Mar. 1
24. γ Cru		1.62	12 28 −56 50	May 10
25. λ Sco	Shaula	1.62	17 30 −37 04	July 25
26. γ Ori	Bellatrix	1.64	5 22 + 6 18	Jan. 25
27. β Tau	El Nath	1.65	5 23 +28 34	Jan. 25
28. β Car	Miaplacidus	1.67	9 13 −69 31	Apr. 1
29. ε Ori	Alnilam	1.70	5 34 − 1 14	Jan. 28
30. ε Car	Avior	1.85	8 21 −59 21	Mar. 10

	DISTANCE (LIGHT-YEARS)	TEMPERATURE (°K)	RADIUS (× SUN'S)	TRUE VISUAL BRIGHTNESS (× SUN'S)
1.	8.7	10,400	1.9	30
2.	100	7,500	35	5,700
3.	38	4,250	35	95
4.	27	9,500	2.4	50
5.	4.3	5,800	1.3	1.3
6.	500	11,200	80	60,000
7.	46	5,000	13	70
8.	11	6,450	2.6	12
9.	73	14,000	4.7	400
10.	190	22,000	22	10,000
11.	16	8,250	1.6	10
12.	300	3,800	1,600	18,000
13.	64	3,900	90	110
14.	190	20,000	11	2,200
15.	220	18,000	4.9	3,000
16.	230	3,500	800	5,600
17.	33	4,100	19	73
18.	23	9,300	1.7	18
19.	500	26,600	43	4,400
20.	1,600	9,500	100	63,000
21.	78	13,000	4	150
22.	330	21,000	16	5,000
23.	47	9,500	1.9	30
24.	60	3,000	200	800
25.	200	20,000	11	2,200
26.	230	21,000	11	2,500
27.	130	12,000	8	400
28.	80	9,500	3	65
29.	900	21,000	40	60,000
30.	330	4,100	100	600

Total and Annular Solar Eclipses

	DATE		TYPE	VISIBILITY
1990	Jan.	26	Annular	Antarctica
	July	22	Total	Finland, Soviet Union, North Pacific
1991	Jan.	15	Annular	Australia, New Zealand
	July	11	Total	Hawaii, Mexico, Colombia
1992	Jan.	4	Annular	Central Pacific Ocean
	June	30	Total	South Atlantic Ocean
1994	May	10	Annular	United States
	Nov.	3	Total	South America, South Atlantic Ocean
1995	Apr.	29	Annular	
	Oct.	24	Total	Iran, India, Southeast Asia, Caroline Islands
1996	——		——	

Lunar Eclipses

DATE			MID-ECLIPSE (E.S.T.)	TYPE
1990	Feb.	9	2:12 p.m.	Total
	Aug.	6	9:07 a.m.	Partial
1991	Dec.	21	5:34 a.m.	Partial
1992	June	14	11:57 p.m.	Partial
	Dec.	9	6:43 p.m.	Total
1993	June	4	8:00 a.m.	Total
	Nov.	29	1:26 a.m.	Total
1994	May	24	10:28 p.m.	Total
1995	Apr.	15	7:17 a.m.	Partial
1996	Apr.	3	7:09 p.m.	Total
	Sept.	26	9:53 p.m.	Total

Almanac of the Planets, 1990-95

This section will help you make a first guess at the identity of planets. You may refine your identification using information in Chapter 3 along with the star finder wheel. Asterisks (*) indicate the occurrence of a planetary conjunction in the list following this section.

	1990		
	EVENING SKY	MIDNIGHT SKY	MORNING SKY
Winter (Jan.–Mar.)	Venus until Jan. 10	Jupiter	Venus (greatest elongation Mar. 30), Mars, Saturn*
Spring (Apr.–June)	Mercury (19° from sun on Apr. 10), Jupiter		Venus, Mars, Saturn
Summer (July–Sept.)	Mercury (27° from sun on Aug. 11)	Saturn	Venus, Mars, Jupiter*
Autumn (Oct.–Dec.)	Mercury (21° from sun on Dec. 5), Venus after Oct. 31, Saturn	Mars	Jupiter

	1991		
	EVENING SKY	MIDNIGHT SKY	MORNING SKY
Winter (Jan.–Mar.)	Mercury (19° from sun on Mar. 25), Mars	Jupiter	Saturn after Jan. 17
Spring (Apr.–June)	Venus (greatest elongation June 12), Mars, Jupiter*		Saturn

	EVENING SKY	MIDNIGHT SKY	MORNING SKY
Summer (July–Sept.)	Mercury (27° from sun on July 21), Venus, Mars, Jupiter until Aug. 17*	Saturn	Venus, Jupiter after Aug. 17*
Autumn (Oct.–Dec.)	Mercury (22° from sun on Nov. 23), Mars until Nov. 7, Saturn		Venus (greatest elongation Nov. 11), Mars after Nov. 8, Jupiter

1992

	EVENING SKY	MIDNIGHT SKY	MORNING SKY
Winter (Jan.–Mar.)	Mercury (18° from sun on Mar. 8), Saturn until Jan. 29	Jupiter	Venus, Mars, Saturn after Jan. 29*
Spring (Apr.–June)	Mercury (26° from sun on June 30), Jupiter		Venus, Mars, Saturn*
Summer (July–Sept.)	Venus, Jupiter until Sept. 17*	Saturn	Mars, Jupiter after Sept. 17
Autumn (Oct.–Dec.)	Mercury (24° from sun on Oct. 30), Venus, Saturn*		Mars, Jupiter

1993

	EVENING SKY	MIDNIGHT SKY	MORNING SKY
Winter (Jan.–Mar.)	Mercury (18° from sun on Feb. 20), Venus (greatest elongation Jan. 21), Saturn until Feb. 8	Mars	Jupiter, Saturn after Feb. 8

	EVENING SKY	MIDNIGHT SKY	MORNING SKY
Spring (Apr.–June)	Mercury (24° from sun on June 11), Mars	Jupiter	Venus (greatest elongation June 11), Saturn
Summer (July–Sept.)	Mars, Jupiter*	Saturn	Venus
Autumn (Oct.–Dec.)	Mercury (24° from sun on Oct. 19), Mars, Saturn*		Venus, Jupiter after Oct. 18

1994

	EVENING SKY	MIDNIGHT SKY	MORNING SKY
Winter (Jan.–Mar.)	Mercury (18° from sun on Feb. 4), Venus, Saturn until Feb 21		Mars, Jupiter, Saturn after Feb. 21*
Spring (Apr.–June)	Mercury (22° from sun on May 24), Venus	Jupiter	Mars, Saturn
Summer (July–Sept.)	Mercury (26° from sun on Sept. 30), Venus (greatest elongation Aug. 22), Jupiter*	Saturn	Mars
Autumn (Oct.–Dec.)	Venus until Nov. 2, Jupiter, Saturn*		Venus after Nov. 2, Mars

1995

	EVENING SKY	MIDNIGHT SKY	MORNING SKY
Winter (Jan.–Mar.)	Mercury (19° from sun on Jan. 20), Saturn until Mar. 5	Mars	Venus (greaest elongation Jan. 13), Jupiter, Saturn after Mar. 5*

	EVENING SKY	MIDNIGHT SKY	MORNING SKY
Spring (Apr.–June)	Mercury (21° from sun on May 7), Mars	Jupiter	Venus, Saturn
Summer (July–Sept.)	Mercury (27° from sun on Sept. 12), Mars, Jupiter	Saturn	Venus until Aug. 17
Autumn (Oct.–Dec.)	Venus, Mars, Jupiter, Saturn*		

CONJUNCTIONS OF VENUS
WITH THE SUN

SUPERIOR CONJUNCTION	INFERIOR CONJUNCTION
Venus switches from a.m. to p.m. sky. Invisible for 2 months on either side. (The phrases "a.m. sky" and "p.m. sky" refer to dawn and evening twilight, respectively.)	Switches from p.m. to a.m. sky. Invisible about 2 weeks on either side.

1990	Nov. 2	Jan. 18
1991	——	Aug. 22
1992	June 13	——
1993	——	Mar. 31
1994	Jan. 17	Nov. 2
1995	Aug. 20	——

CONJUNCTIONS OF OUTER PLANETS
WITH THE SUN

Planets are invisible for several weeks on either side of these conjunctions.

YEAR	MARS	JUPITER	SATURN
1990	—	July 14	Jan. 6
1991	Nov. 7	Aug. 17	Jan. 17
1992	—	Sept. 17	Jan. 29
1993	Dec. 26	Oct. 18	Feb. 8
1994	—	Nov. 17	Feb. 21
1995	—	Dec. 18	Mar. 5
1996	Mar. 4	—	Mar. 17
1997	—	Jan. 19	Mar. 30

PLANETARY CONJUNCTIONS

When two planets arrive at the same point of the zodiac, they are said to be in conjunction. Astronomically, there is nothing particularly significant about conjunctions, but they can be a pretty sight. The following list contains the most interesting groupings during the coming years. All dates are approximate, as the events (excluding the moon's position) usually last for several days.

1990

Feb. 1:	Venus, Mercury, Saturn, Mars in the a.m. sky
Feb. 21:	Venus, Mars, Saturn with the old moon and Uranus and Neptune (invisible). See chart.
Mar. 22:	Similar to Feb. 21
Aug. 12:	Venus, Jupiter in a.m. sky

1991

June 15:	Venus, Mars, Jupiter with new moon in p.m. sky
July 12:	Mercury, Venus, Mars, Jupiter in p.m. sky. See chart.
Sept. 6:	Mercury, Venus, Jupiter with new moon in a.m. sky

1992

Mar. 1:	Venus, Mars, Saturn with old moon in a.m. sky
Mar. 12:	Moon very close to Saturn (occultation seen in Europe)
Apr. 26:	Mercury, Venus, Mars, Saturn in a.m. sky
Aug. 29:	Venus, Jupiter with new moon in p.m. sky
Dec. 27:	Venus, Saturn with new moon in p.m. sky

1993

Aug. 20:	Mars close to Jupiter in p.m. sky for next few weeks
Sept. 16:	Mercury, Mars, Jupiter in p.m. sky with new moon
Nov. 12:	Mercury, Venus, Jupiter with old moon in a.m. sky

1994

Mar. 9–25:	Mercury, Mars, Saturn in a.m. sky
Sept. 7:	Mercury, Venus, Jupiter, Spica with new moon in p.m. sky. See chart.
Oct. 7:	Similar to previous month's event

1995

Jan. 14:	Mars, Jupiter in a.m. sky
Mar. 13:	Venus, Saturn in very close conjunction in a.m. sky
Oct. 25:	Venus, Mars, Jupiter with new moon in p.m. sky
Nov. 23:	Repeat of previous month's event
Dec. 25:	Mercury, Venus, Mars, Saturn, Uranus (binoculars), Neptune (invisible) with new moon in p.m. sky

Phases of the Moon, 1990–95

	1990				1991			
	NEW		FULL		NEW		FULL	
Jan.	26^d	19^h	11^d	5^h	15^d	24^h	30	6
Feb.	25	9	9	19	14	18	28	18
Mar.	26	20	11	11	16	5	30	7
Apr.	25	4	10	3	14	20	28	21
May	24	12	9	20	14	5	28	12
June	22	19	8	11	12	12	27	3
July	22	3	8	1	11	19	26	18
Aug.	20	13	6	14	10	2	25	9
Sept.	19	1	5	2	8	11	23	23
Oct.	18	16	4	12	7	22	23	11
Nov.	17	9	2	22	6	11	21	23
Dec.	17	4	2	8	6	4	21	10
	—	—	31	19	—	—	—	—

	1992				1993			
	NEW		FULL		NEW		FULL	
Jan.	4^d	23^h	19^d	21^h	22^d	18^h	8^d	13^h
Feb.	3	19	18	8	21	13	6	24
Mar.	4	13	18	18	23	7	8	10
Apr.	3	5	17	5	21	24	6	19
May	2	18	16	16	21	14	6	4
June	1	4	15	5	20	2	4	13
	30	12	—	—	—	—	—	—

	1992				1993			
	NEW		FULL		NEW		FULL	
July	29	20	14	19	19	11	3	24
Aug.	28d	3h	13d	10h	17d	19h	2d	12h
Sept.	26	11	12	2	16	3	1	3
	—	—	—	—	—	—	30	19
Oct.	25	21	11	18	15	12	31	13
Nov.	24	9	10	9	13	22	29	6
Dec.	24	1	10	0	13	9	28	23

	1994				1995			
	NEW		FULL		NEW		FULL	
Jan.	11d	23h	27d	13h	1d	11h	16d	20h
	—	—	—	—	31	23	—	—
Feb.	10	15	26	1	—	—	15	12
Mar.	12	7	27	11	1	12	17	1
	—	—	—	—	31	2	—	—
Apr.	11	0	25	20	30	18	15	12
May	10	17	25	4	29	9	14	21
June	9	8	23	12	28	1	13	4
July	8	22	22	20	27	15	12	11
Aug.	7	9	21	7	26	5	10	18
Sept.	5	19	19	20	24	17	9	4
Oct.	5	4	19	12	24	5	8	16
Nov.	3	14	18	7	22	16	7	7
Dec.	2	24	18	2	22	2	7	1

The times given are days and hours at the longitude of Greenwich, England. For other longitudes, subtract one hour for each 15 west or add one hour for each 15 east. In the U.S., subtract 5 hours for E.S.T., 6 hours for C.S.T., etc., or 4 hours for E.D.T., 5 hours for C.D.T., etc.

A NOTE ABOUT THE AUTHOR

Charles Allen Whitney was born in Milwaukee, Wisconsin, in 1929. After receiving a B.S. in physics from the Massachusetts Institute of Technology, Whitney completed his M.A. and Ph.D. in astronomy at Harvard University. He has been a physicist at the Smithsonian Astrophysical Observatory since 1956, and is a professor emeritus of astronomy at Harvard. The Discovery of Our Galaxy *was published by Knopf in 1971. He is married, the father of five children, grandfather of several, and lives in Weston, Massachusetts.*

A NOTE ON THE TYPE

This book was set in Caledonia, a Linotype face designed by W. A. Dwiggins. It belongs to the family of printing types called "modern face" by printers—a term used to mark the change in style of type letters that occurred about 1800. Caledonia borders on the general design of Scotch Modern, but is more freely drawn than that letter.

Composed, printed, and bound by
The Haddon Craftsmen, Inc., Scranton, Pennsylvania.
Based on a design by The Etheredges.